THEODORE G. GROVE
Portland State University

Experiences in Interpersonal Communication

Prentice-Hall, Inc., Englewood Cliffs, New Jersey

Library of Congress Cataloging in Publication Data

GROVE, THEODORE G.
   Experiences in interpersonal communication.

   1. Interpersonal relations.   2. Communication.
I. Title.
HM132.G77   301.14   75-22296
ISBN 0-13-294975-X

© 1976 by PRENTICE-HALL, Inc., *Englewood Cliffs, New Jersey*

Printed in the United States of America

10   9   8   7   6   5   4   3   2   1

PRENTICE-HALL INTERNATIONAL, INC., *London*
PRENTICE-HALL OF AUSTRALIA, PTY. LTD, *Sydney*
PRENTICE-HALL OF CANADA, LTD., *Toronto*
PRENTICE-HALL OF INDIA PRIVATE LIMITED, *New Delhi*
PRENTICE-HALL OF JAPAN, INC., *Tokyo*
PRENTICE-HALL OF SOUTHEAST ASIA (PTE.) LTD., *Singapore*

PRENTICE-HALL SERIES IN SPEECH COMMUNICATION
Larry L. Barker and Robert J. Kibler,
Consulting Editors

Experiences in Interpersonal Communication
Theodore G. Grove

The Great American Communication Catalogue
Irving J. Rein

Group Communication: Discussion, Processes, and Applications
Alvin A. Goldberg and Carl E. Larson

Language: Concepts and Processes
Joseph A. DeVito

Living Communication
Abne M. Eisenberg

Mass News: Practices, Controversies, and Alternatives
David J. LeRoy and Christopher H. Sterling

Monologue to Dialogue: An Exploration of Interpersonal Communication
Charles T. Brown and Paul W. Keller

Organizing A Speech: A Programmed Guide
Judy L. Haynes

Perspectives on Communication in Social Conflict
Gerald R. Miller and Herbert W. Simons

Persuasion: Communication in Social Conflict
Raymond S. Ross

The Prospect of Rhetoric
Lloyd F. Bitzer and Edwin Black

Speech Communication: Fundamentals and Practice, third edition
Raymond S. Ross

Transracial Communication
Arthur L. Smith

FOR ZEE

Contents

II
METHODS FOR STUDYING INTERPERSONAL COMMUNICATION

A
Simple Observation   47

B
Active Intervention   94

C
Instrumented Feedback   99

C

Individual First Aid   **145**

D

Group First Aid   **153**

E

Continuations

IV

STRATEGIES FOR GROUP PROBLEM-SOLVING

A

Problem-Solving Procedures   **165**

B
Problem-Solving Attitudes **174**

C
Special Problems **190**

D
Continuations

Preface

This book is intended to help its user inquire into interpersonal communication. High school or university student, corporate or governmental employee, businessman or industrial worker, craftsman or cosmetologist, doctor, dentist, attorney, or clerk can find it useful. The material has been designed for anyone who feels the need to improve his or her understanding of—and skill in—interpersonal communication, that is, in two-person or small group communication.

The structure of the book allows little or no supervision. Yet it can also function, of course, as a classroom guide to learning experiences in communication for those of us who are called "teacher." To that end, the book provides a plethora of material from which instruction units may be selected in keeping with the teacher's own special approaches to the subject matter.

Instructors generally agree that the traditional classroom lecture method has a very limited application to subjects with behavioral objectives, such as face-to-face communication skills. One must have immediate access to concrete communication experiences for maximum learning to occur. Reading about and talking about communication processes are not enough. Instructors are now employing a variety of approaches that are designed to capitalize on a communication experience and make of it a learning experience. These approaches include outside observations, intensive group experiences, focused demonstrations, role-playing, problem simulations, and games. Common to all of these methods is the goal of exploring communication concepts and theories through communication experiences. The book serves the gamut of approaches suggested above with a set of experience units devoted to some of the most important concepts and processes within interpersonal communication.

We are constrained by the recent fad in communication resource publications to state that this is definitely not a book of "fun and games." Although we hope that many of the units are "fun," only seven of the eighty could be construed as "games." These are labeled as such. A unit was included or excluded on the basis of one criterion: "Does it elicit the kind of behavior that is stressed by theorists of the interpersonal communication process?"

With only three exceptions, noted in the text, each of the units stands alone as an experience unit without regard to the others. The units are aimed at different levels of user sophistication, ranging from the beginning student to the research-minded graduate student; with respect to the graduate student, portions of Section II provide techniques for inquiry and discovery. All units are written for a general readership, though many suggest applications that have potential for the investigator of interpersonal communication phenomena.

As with many books from academe, this one too "just happened." Originally, none of this material was planned for publication. The various units were developed over the last ten years in the communication classroom. Every one of them has been revised and tested again inside and outside of the classroom by a heterogeneity of learners. Most have evolved through several different applications and forms into the present version. Instructions were written to supplant our "talking face" from time to time as we attempted to present selected experiences in communication. In a sense, we think of this material as a portable instructor, a "do-some-of-it-yourself kit," that puts a greater share of commitment and initiative where it belongs—into the hands of the student of communication. At the same time, it frees instructors to concentrate on their learning goals in as many other ways as they like to employ.

Acknowledgments

In such a work, acknowledgments are never extended broadly enough. Who is to recall the countless influences and suggestions made over the years by colleagues and students alike? First, twelve students from a beginning class in "Communication within Groups" at Portland State University provided the impetus I needed to begin translating scattered notes and ragtag dittos into organized prose. They are Karen Tufford, David Kleine, Donald Taylor, III, Herbert Halstead, Mathew Klein, Carey Franham, Linda Tozer, James Waters, Grant Cummings, Darlene Peterson, Jack Mongeon, and Jack Sieforth. Together, we discussed ideas for some of the major structural divisions of this book and the initial version of about six of the units that appear here. Interaction with inventive colleagues like David Butt and Gerry Phillips of Pennsylvania State University, Paul Friedman of the University of Kansas, and Stanley Jones of the University of Colorado has certainly had an incalculable influence on my orientation to learning and discovery. Loretta Malandro of Florida State University went far beyond the call of her honorarium in the bang-up review she did on the first manuscript. A substantial acknowledgment must also go to interpersonal communication itself. It has been through this process that my students and I have tried to discover for ourselves the means to fashion communicative events and experiences as raw material for our inquiries.

T.G.G.

Experiences
in
Interpersonal
Communication

Introduction

WHAT IT IS

The eighty units in this book have been devised to assist you in learning about interpersonal communication. Instructions within the units enable you—with a little help from your friends—to complete them on your own, if you want to. To gain insight and skill about your own communication and that of others, it is helpful to be able to experience a particular behavior when you are putting forth your efforts to *understand* that behavior. Within each unit, therefore, you will be guided toward some form of communicative behavior. You will then be asked for thoughtful analysis or ideas about the experience.

It is impossible, of course, for an academician to write a book of exercises concerning his specialty without encumbering it with his particular theoretical biases. We have done our best, nonetheless, to present experiential forms that support widely diverging theoretical points of view and learning strategies. The goal here is simply to help you understand the elusive processes of interpersonal communication in a learning space that is not bounded by three walls and a blackboard. The processes are not easy to master. I invite you to join our company in exploiting every avenue and perhaps some "blind alleys" as well to that end.

HOW TO USE IT

Throughout the experience units, the words "READ FOCUS" and "DO ACTIVITY" jut out to the left of the text. They are a signal to read the introductory orienting material and to translate directions into activities. The READ/ DO sequence of each unit proceeds through a step-by-step development of that unit. The brief descriptive phrases of "FOCUS" serve to underscore the purpose of the exercise. In some cases a lengthy explanation accompanies these phrases and has been set off in a bracketed paragraph or paragraphs. The end of each experience unit is cleverly signaled by the word "END."

The units follow rather closely one of two basic formats. More than two-thirds have a straightforward didactic structure. You are introduced to the unit. You are guided through its major activities. And, finally, you are asked to "DO FEEDBACK" or "DO ANALYSIS" of what has taken place. The other format, scattered unequally throughout the four sections of the book, is inductively structured. In these units you are thrust into an activity with only a brief introductory focus statement. You are then directed to a page near the end of that section for instructions on completion of that unit under "DO APPLICATION." Maximum value can be obtained from these units by maintaining a policy of "no peeky."

All units are coded for personnel and time requirements immediately below and to the right of the exercise title as follows:

A = Alone. For the individual working alone.

SA = Start Alone. Must be initiated by one person, but requires eventual cooperation of a small group.

D = Dyad. Pertains to two people, so the initiator will need a partner.

G = Group. May be initiated by a small group.

G+ = Groups. Requires coordination among several small groups; works best with the aid of a coordinator.

S = Short. Will take from ten to thirty minutes to complete.

L = Long. Will take from forty to sixty minutes to complete.

E = Extended. May not be completed on one occasion.

Many of the units fit more than one personnel or time requirement and are multicoded accordingly. A glance at the code on several pages will illustrate this simple system. After that, you will need only to look at the code of a unit to determine if you have the human and time resources needed to complete it.

Your decisions in selecting units can be informed by checking three sources of information: (1) the lettered subsection description in the contents (2) the focus statement beginning each unit; and (3) the four section introductions below. Several factors should be kept in mind in your selection decisions:

Extent. It is neither likely nor desirable that all or even nearly all the units be completed in a term, or in a semester. Initial sampling for familiarity, followed by an informed, careful selection or rejection of units is, therefore, the best procedure to follow.

Range of Difficulty.   Some units are relatively simple and easy in their form and in the behavior they require. Others are rather complex and demanding. Because of organizational demands, the units could not be arranged solely in order of difficulty. Consequently, the user must try to avoid mismatching his preparation with the level of unit difficulty. This will require the user to skip around and select units very carefully.

Timing.   Relationships between work partners and group members must be more fully developed for some units than for others. For example, familiarity and a certain amount of trust are prerequisite to experience units involving frank evaluations of oneself or others or both.

Order.   The order in which either sections or units may be used is completely flexible. It should be determined by your needs and the factors just discussed. Do not be coerced into a serial progression from front to back merely on the basis of section placement in the book. You may prefer to skip around from section to section, following units on a commonality discovered on your own. To gain familiarity with the arrangement of units available, read the four section introductions below before proceeding further.

INTRODUCTION TO SECTION I

The units of Section I, "Explorations in Interpersonal Communication," range across a broad spectrum of topics and concepts. Their emphasis, nevertheless, is on discovery and awareness. Certain aspects of interpersonal communication you are already familiar with because of your past experiences. But this section also introduces new communicative experiences at several levels. Units focus on a variety of issues and are aimed at one's awareness of concepts and processes. They deal with, among other things, awareness of one's own communicative behavior and that of others. They are also concerned with one's awareness of language and nonverbal characteristics, of language barriers to communication, and some issues for small groups.

INTRODUCTION TO SECTION II

The second section, "Methods for Studying Interpersonal Communication," contains units that introduce some tools and perspectives for observing and investigating interpersonal communication. Central to learning about anything are the questions, "How can I begin to study it?" "Where do I start?" This section is concerned with ways of finding out about interpersonal communication. Approaches to discovery, techniques and instruments for observation, questions of evaluating what you have observed, and attitudes of investigation are the issues around which these units revolve.

We are forever drawing conclusions and making evaluations in our experiences with one another. Yet, we rarely have the luxury of pausing to consider the processes that we go through when we observe others. Nor do we usually have the opportunity to consider the validity of our casual conclusions by comparing notes with others who are going through the same motions. Here, we take the time to ask questions that perhaps we have not yet considered in connection with our evaluations and conclusions, and we try to provide practical methods for obtaining some answers.

Some units describe how to make and use such instruments as rating scales, interaction analysis profiles, and content analysis schemes. Other units concentrate on how observers can provide feedback about group processes. Still others pertain to the methods for studying particular aspects of interpersonal communication.

You will not necessarily become proficient with all methods in every unit. Some are more difficult to execute successfully than others. Studying face-to-face communication is an art and, like any art, must be practiced until judgment and technique are highly developed. Each of these experiences should be considered as first-time attempts at using methods, some of which can provide the basis for follow-up practice and refinement. Such systematic studies can produce an understanding far superior and much more useful than the casual and hurried perceptions of raw experience.

INTRODUCTION TO SECTION III

"Approaches to Changing Communication Behavior," the focus of Section III, goes beyond mere awareness and understanding and takes up ideas for changing one's habits and responses in communication. Some of the units in Section III deal with changing one's own communicative behavior and some address the problem of helping others effect changes in theirs. An awareness of what is going on within face-to-face communication is of little value if that information is not somehow used to improve the quality of subsequent interaction. You are actively involved in this section with strategies for changing behavior. Although the units do not depend in any specific way on the preceding sections, I and II, the communicator with some insight into "how things got that way" is naturally in a better position to (1) understand the dynamics of changing communicative behavior and (2) produce some of the changes he seeks to bring about.

Our philosophy in presenting the material in this section requires that we reject two extreme points of view concerning the changing of human behavior. The first school of thought maintains that one needs to pay money (a kind of ritual) to psychiatrists, universities, counselors, and special teachers or gurus in order to achieve any real or long-lasting progress toward solving problems of

communication—the more money, the higher the expectations. Not coincidental-
ly, where the dollar cost is the greatest, many are all too ready to label communication problems as "psychiatric," without regard to the nature of training of a
given psychiatrist or psychotherapist. "Why shouldn't my problems go away?"
they ask indignantly. "Look how much I'm paying for them!" The opposite
viewpoint—that change in deep-seated problems and habits of a lifetime can be
easily and effortlessly remedied—is equally false. Sometimes even the slightest
behavioral change requires a tremendous personal commitment and all the help
one can get from others. Fortunately, most people continue to grapple with
their own problems of self-improvement with the aid of all the sources available.

Every day of our lives others are trying to change every imaginable facet of
our behavior: what kind of food we should eat, what kind of chemicals we
should put into our bodies, what candidates we should elect, what cars we should
drive, what political or religious or governmental loyalties we should have, what
headache tablets we should swallow, what hair spray we should use, what we
should do with our spare time, what or whom we should love or hate, what kind
of clothes we should put on our backs. The list is almost limitless. Most of us do
not have the advantage of putting the expensive media like television, radio,
newspapers, and magazines to use in our efforts to alter the behavior of others.
For this reason it is all the more important that we develop some appreciation
and some skill in achieving change through the one medium we all do possess—
the medium of interpersonal communication.

Even if we were not the targets of change, we would still have reason to
inquire into methods for changing others' minds and behavior through oral communication. In a world where we must frequently work together to get things
done, individuals who have studied the art of communicating with people to
achieve common goals will be more likely to achieve them than those who have
not. They will be better able to "make a difference." Further, if one is aware of
certain approaches for changing the communicative behavior of others, one is
more likely to recognize the approaches that may occasionally be directed
against oneself. Moreover, if a person has some facility with changing others, he
or she is better able to understand similar efforts by others. Effecting this kind
of equalization in our interpersonal encounters is important, for only then can
we obtain a full interplay of ideas and base our decisions and actions on the relative quality of those ideas.

The units in Section III are aimed at habituated ways of perceiving problems, people, and events; at rigid, uncreative group norms and procedures; at
styles of leadership; and at communicator roles. Some exercises seek to eliminate
a specific barrier to communication among individuals. Other units deal with
changes that facilitate small group effectiveness.

Changing human behavior, one's own or others', is always an ambitious
undertaking and is usually sprinkled with liberal doses of disappointment and
failure. An attitude of realism at the beginning can provide a kind of armor

against these disillusionments. Even more than the mastering of observational techniques of Section II, facilitating change is a delicate art. Cultivation is time-consuming and attaining proficiency is difficult. The best practitioners have developed their skill over a lifetime. It is also hard to generalize about what is successful with one person, one group, one task, or one situation in connection with other persons, groups, tasks, and situations. When attempting to change human behavior, timing is extremely important, sensitivity to the moods and perceptions of others is crucial, and a refined awareness of the impact of one's own behavior is mandatory.

INTRODUCTION TO SECTION IV

Section IV, "Strategies for Group Problem-Solving," involves you in procedures that have specific application to problem-solving communication within a small group. Whenever people get together to make a decision or tackle a problem, each person usually brings with him a number of assumptions concerning what procedures to follow, what to attack first, what kind of controls should or should not be imposed on member contributions, what method should or should not be used to resolve differences of opinion and so forth. All too often these assumptions—these habituated ways of thinking about how a group should go about solving its problems—severely limit the communicators to a single approach in their deliberations. For example, most people believe that conflict of all kinds is to be avoided, that it is a hindrance to the progress of the group's work. Because of such attitudes, many opportunities to use conflict creatively to advance group goals are missed.

Probably the most unfortunate aspect of the way most problem-solving groups operate is their single-mindedness in sticking to the first method that they decide to adopt. A headlong rush to deal with the task obscures alternatives that might work better. Many times a group task is a collection of interrelated subtasks. This kind of problem necessitates a little thought about alternative approaches and also a willingness to experiment a bit with group methods. Such challenges require an attitude of flexibility and tentativeness that many group members do not think to entertain.

The biggest asset a group facing a challenging task can have is members with the willingness to suspend some of their assumptions for the sake of finding a better way. Strong wills must give way to fresh thinking if people are to do the very best they can in their problem-solving attempts. Units in Section IV, therefore, open up some avenues of escape for the traps into which many of us fall. They are designed to start you thinking about and doing some things you would not ordinarily think about or do in your small groups. The valuable resources of analytical and creative thought that reside within all group members are useless if the group's methods fail to reach its members and engage their skills and resources. There are ways of tapping the resources of group members that many of us have never considered.

The units of this section also emphasize special problems including the differentiation of group tasks, how to resolve disagreements, special roles that help, the creative use of conflict, and how to find a common ground. When one is aware of the variety of methods and approaches available to group members, it is difficult indeed to remain dogmatic about problem-solving procedures. It is hoped that this section will add to the sophistication necessary for the experimental and selective application of methods within the small group.

You are now ready to select a point of departure and explore with us the processes of interpersonal communication.

I

Explorations in Interpersonal Communication

A

The Communicator

1. YOUR OWN WORLD

G   G+   S

READ FOCUS: Close communication relationships.

DO ACTIVITY: Take a sheet of paper, turn it sideways on your desk, and number "1" through "5" down the left-hand margin. Write the names of your five closest friends (three or four will do). These may not be relatives, but should be the persons to whom you feel the closest.

WHEN FINISHED, GO TO PAGE __35__ TO COMPLETE THIS UNIT.

2. BEFORE/AFTER

A   D   E

READ FOCUS: Impressions of others. Information bases for judging others.

DO ACTIVITY: About the end of your first week of contact with an individual, write a paragraph summing up your impressions of that person's communicative behavior—both strong and weak points, but whatever you perceive. Call it as you see it. Seal the paragraph in an envelope, label it, and give it to the instructor (or a friend). In the last week of class or after several months of contact with the person, write another paragraph summing up your impressions about his communicative behavior. Present it to the instructor (or friend) and he will return your sealed envelope containing the first paragraph. Compare them.

DO FEEDBACK: Communicate all or any portion of your two paragraphs to your partner at the end of the term and he will reciprocate. Can you draw any conclusions about the way in which people generally process information about other individuals? How they form impressions? How the impressions, once formed, influence their communicative behavior with that individual? How impressions influence *your* communicative behavior?

END

3.   AS IF

A   D   G   S   L

READ FOCUS: Exploration of the knowledge process known as "empathy." Working toward achieving some degree of empathy with others; for example: group members.

[Little is known about the ability to put oneself in the place of another, to see the world as someone else sees it, to interact with a real feeling for the feelings of the "other." But we do know that the more empathy one possesses, the better communicator that person usually is. This exercise should help the student understand empathy—as a process and as a tool to foster better interpersonal relationships, thereby improving communication with specific others.]

DO ACTIVITY: Respond with a short written paragraph to each of the following in as thoughtful a way as you can.

Think how you and your life might be changed or different if you were:

1.   A member of the opposite sex.
2.   A poor Irish farmer.
3.   A Catholic priest.
4.   A sixty-nine-year old widow or widower with no children.
5.   An inmate in a penitentiary with twenty years to serve.
6.   A six-year-old child being raised by you.

Now take each member of your group, one at a time, and think *as if* you were that person. What might life be like for you? What might the group be like for you?

DO ANALYSIS: Speculate on your empathic ability. Is it high? Low? Average? Why do you think so? Discuss and compare your responses with those of others. How might increased capacity for empathy improve your communicative effectiveness?

END

4.   FOR KEEPS

G   G+   S

READ FOCUS: Exploring individual differences among communicators.

DO ACTIVITY: Without any discussion, remove all coins from your pockets and purses, placing whatever you have on the surface before you. Take a minute to look around you, noting where others are sitting. The name of this game is "For Keeps." In a moment you will all rise, circulate around the room, and distribute your money in any amount to whomever and however many others you wish. You will put your money on the surface in front of where the other person or persons had been sitting. When you are through, return to your chair and check:

1.   How much you received from others.
2.   If you have any left from your original amount.

Reread these directions and begin.

WHEN FINISHED, GO TO PAGE   36   TO COMPLETE THIS UNIT.

5.   SELF SYMBOL

D   G   S

READ FOCUS: Communication of highly personal and complex feelings; a practice situation.

DO ACTIVITY: Find an object that is small enough to carry without much difficulty—one that tells you a great deal about "who you are." The object should be one that symbolizes your selfhood in the broadest possible way—one that communicates who you are to yourself. Bring this object to some people who do not know you very well. Take five minutes in an attempt to explain as effectively as you can the nature of your "relating" to that object—why it is a symbol of your "self."

DO FEEDBACK: After your five-minute explanation, elicit reactions from your listeners regarding what they know about you now that they did not know before, what aspect of your remarks were effective communication, and what aspect of your remarks were ineffective communication. Discuss.

END

B

Interaction Process

6.   FRONT-TO-FRONT DYADS

D   G+   S

READ FOCUS: Drawing inferences about another. "Sizing up." The acquaintance process.

DO ACTIVITY: Sit with someone with whom you have not interacted. *Do not
talk*! We are going to do something now that we usually do at a distance and
covertly. Look at your partner. Again, *do not talk*! Just look at your partner
and size him or her up. Fix a firm impression of your partner in your mind.
Got it? Now, privately, respond in writing (in the space provided on the following page) to the following four items.

1.   Write the first word or phrase that comes to mind that best sums up your
     partner.
2.   Write the word or phrase that you think your partner picked for you. That
     is, try to guess what your partner wrote down for Item 1.
3.   List briefly all the ways in which you guess that you are probably similar to
     and different from your partner in personality—as a communicator, as a
     leader, as a sports fan, as a thinker, dancer, or anything else.
4.   Make some guesses about what your partner might have put for Item 3.

"Size Up" Notes

1.

2.

3.

4.

When you have both finished writing, close this book, forget what you have written, and chat for a few minutes about the class itself or any other subject that comes to mind—*except* what you have just written. After five minutes, stop. Turn your paper up again and reread what you have written, making any changes; additions, deletions, or modifications you wish to make.

WHEN FINISHED, GO TO PAGE ___37___ TO COMPLETE THIS UNIT.

7.   IDENTITY DRAW

G   S

READ FOCUS: Identity. Impact on others.

DO ACTIVITY: Write on one slip of paper three adjectives or verbs that might help someone who did not know you very well to identify you—words that describe how you probably "come across" to others. Do not use references to physical attributes—only attributes of behavior and personality. Then without revealing what you have written to anyone in your group, turn your paper face down.

WHEN FINISHED, GO TO PAGE ___37___ TO COMPLETE THIS UNIT.

8.   FANTASY DIALOGUE

D   S

READ FOCUS: Anticipating interaction. "Sizing up."

DO ACTIVITY: Pick a partner with whom you have not talked before. *Do not talk*! Sit down close to one another. We are going to do something again that we usually do covertly and at a distance. It may be uncomfortable, but it is essential that you remain silent.

1. Look the partner over. Take a minute and just look.
2. Now, close your eyes (both of you). In a minute you are going to chat together. But now, with your eyes closed, try to anticipate how your conversation might go. Try to fantasize what you might say. Create a dialogue. Try to imagine how your partner might react, what you and your partner might feel, how the encounter in general will proceed, including its mood and pace. Work on this fantasy for three minutes.
3. Open your eyes. Without talking, write down the dominant themes or images of your fantasy. That is, write down those elements of your fantasy that are strong enough for you to remember.
4. Turn your notes face down and forget about them. Chat with your partner about anything, but *not* about this exercise or your fantasy. Converse for five minutes.

WHEN FINISHED, GO TO PAGE   38   TO COMPLETE THIS UNIT.

9.   ROTATING DYADS

G+   L

READ FOCUS: Interdependence between communicators. Adaptation to the other.

[Regardless of how specific or well-defined your communicative goal, the variability of others' reactions is so great and so unpredictable that the unexpected is the rule, and our half-planned communicative goals are upset as often as not. When we begin to interact, we never really know where our dialogue is going to take us. How the other person will influence our dialogue is always a mystery until it happens.]

DO ACTIVITY: Divide a large group into two equal subgroups—a "Lobby Group" and a "Partner Group."

Partner Group: Arrange yourselves in a circle in the middle of the room. Sit down in equally spaced chairs, each some distance from your closest neighbor. Before being seated, place an empty chair next to yours on the outer rim of the circle. As shown in Figure 1 below, partner chairs are designated "X" and empty chairs are designated "O."

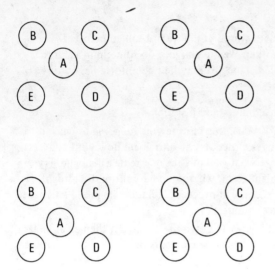

FIGURE 1.   Chair Arrangement

Lobby Group: Individually, think of a communicative goal that you would like to pursue for a few minutes—something you feel strongly about. It could involve explaining a special interest, a hobby, or something in the news. Write a brief statement describing this goal on a slip of paper and put it in your pocket, then seat yourself in one of the empty chairs next to a partner. Discuss your topic with your partner for exactly three minutes and stop. Now rotate clockwise along with other lobbyists to the next partner. Talk with your new partner about your topic for three minutes and repeat the process five or six times.

WHEN FINISHED, GO TO PAGE   39   TO COMPLETE THIS UNIT.

10.   RESPONSE PREDICTION

                                                                    D   S

READ FOCUS: Empathy. Feedback on another's view of your self-concept. Judging others.

[There is one area of agreement among those who study the difficult, elusive quality termed "empathy": it is a quality possessed in large measure by the most effective communicators. To have empathy is to estimate, with some accuracy, how another person feels, thinks, reacts. It is different from sympathy. To have empathy for another, you need not agree with their feelings or ideas (although you might in a given case); you need only understand some things about how the other person does feel and think. A high degree of empathy is usually accompanied by a considerable potential for role-playing, although being a skilled role player does not necessarily insure that one is highly empathic. In short, empathy is an ability to relate psychologically to other individuals or, to parrot a cliche, to "walk in the shoes of another." The best indicator of one's empathic level is probably one's success in predicting the responses of others. Here, we will not claim to *measure* empathy in any but a general sense. However, we will tinker with it a bit and in the process receive some feedback concerning another's estimation of our own self-concept.]

DO ACTIVITY: Pair off with someone that you do not know extremely well but with whom you have interacted a bit. Separate from all others and sit down together. *Do not talk.* Both of you fill out the seven-point Response Prediction Ratings Sheet on pages 21 and 23 as follows:

1. Respond to each of the eleven items by placing an "X" in one of the seven spaces separating the adjective pairs in a manner that represents your feelings about *yourself*—about how *you* are in general. In other words, on the form labeled "Myself," describe yourself by checking nearer to one or the other of the adjectives. Indicate a number for all eleven items.

2. On the second sheet, use an "O" to indicate your guess on how your *partner* responded to each item in his or her self-description. In other words, put your "O" where you think your partner put an "X." Do this for all eleven items.

3. Compute your partner's *accuracy score* by determining how close your partner came to estimating your responses. Use the column heading numbers (1 through 7) to determine the distance between *your* X (your sheet) and your *partner's* O (his sheet). Mark a difference score for each item in the left-hand column, total all eleven of these, and note this total on your partner's sheet. The result represents how accurately or inaccurately your partner estimated your self-description responses. For example:

	Difference Score	*1 2 3 4 5 6 7*
Item 1	2	O X
Item 2	4	X O
Total Difference	6	

DO FEEDBACK: When you are done, compare your "empathy scores" with each other and with other dyads. Low scores reflect high empathy. There are usually differences—sometimes large differences—among individuals in their ability to predict the responses of others. Discuss item by item how you described yourself, your partner's predictions, where you were right or wrong, and why.

Report any interesting observations from your dyad to the class.

END

RESPONSE PREDICTION RATINGS SHEET

MYSELF *(Use "X")*

Partner's
Difference
Scores

		1	2	3	4	5	6	7	
___	OUTWARD	—	—	—	—	—	—	—	INWARD
___	QUIET	—	—	—	—	—	—	—	LOUD
___	STRONG	—	—	—	—	—	—	—	WEAK
___	PASSIVE	—	—	—	—	—	—	—	ACTIVE
___	INDEPENDENT	—	—	—	—	—	—	—	DEPENDENT
___	WARM	—	—	—	—	—	—	—	COLD
___	SAD	—	—	—	—	—	—	—	HAPPY
___	DELIBERATE	—	—	—	—	—	—	—	SPONTANEOUS
___	SOFT	—	—	—	—	—	—	—	HARD
___	KNOWING	—	—	—	—	—	—	—	WONDERING
___	ORGANIZED	—	—	—	—	—	—	—	CHAOTIC

_____ Total

PREDICTION OF OTHER'S RESPONSES (Use "O")

	1	2	3	4	5	6	7	
OUTWARD	—	—	—	—	—	—	—	INWARD
QUIET	—	—	—	—	—	—	—	LOUD
STRONG	—	—	—	—	—	—	—	WEAK
PASSIVE	—	—	—	—	—	—	—	ACTIVE
INDEPENDENT	—	—	—	—	—	—	—	DEPENDENT
WARM	—	—	—	—	—	—	—	COLD
SAD	—	—	—	—	—	—	—	HAPPY
DELIBERATE	—	—	—	—	—	—	—	SPONTANEOUS
SOFT	—	—	—	—	—	—	—	HARD
KNOWING	—	—	—	—	—	—	—	WONDERING
ORGANIZED	—	—	—	—	—	—	—	CHAOTIC

11.   SOUNDS OF SILENCE

G   S

READ FOCUS: The many meanings of silence. Speech as noise.

DO ACTIVITY: Persuade your group to sit quietly together in the usual seating positions used when working on a group task. Do *not* talk or engage in any nervous physical activity such as doodling, pencil tapping, etc. Just sit and suffer silence for five whole minutes, all the while looking at one another as you do when talking together. Avoid a head-down position and resist the urge to avoid eye contact with other group members. Before starting, appoint someone to inform the group when five minutes have elapsed so there will be no need for participants to glance at their wristwatch or other available timepiece. Begin.

DO ANALYSIS: Discuss your feelings and explain them. Consider the following questions in your reflections:

How much of vocal utterance is really for the purpose of communication and how much is simply an outlet for the expression of anxieties, for the easing of tension and personal uneasiness? How much of what we say is mistaken for attempts at communication by ourselves and by our listeners when it is not really the product of our specific *communicative* motives or goals? What can we recognize in our own utterances that has little to do with communication? What did silence mean to you here? What thoughts did you have at the time? What meanings can silence have during attempted communication—long pauses, for instance? How could you employ silence more effectively as an aid to communication? Personally? In the group?

END

C

The Small Group

12.   RANK DIFFERENCES₁

G   S

READ FOCUS: Characteristics of group members. Sensitivity to the needs of others.

DO ACTIVITY: Listed below are certain characteristics, or dimensions, concerning which group members quite often differ from one another. Factors such as these can be especially important in influencing, for better or worse, the nature of a group experience and even affect how well the members get along, how much they achieve, and how much or how little satisfaction they derive from the group. Privately, rank order (from 1 to 6) these dimensions on the basis of how important each seems to be in making your group whatever it is at this point. A "1" is "most influential"; a "6" is "least influential."

_____ Language style and vocabulary

_____ Responsiveness to needs of others

_____ Talkativeness

_____ Nonverbal mannerisms

_____ Apparent level of motivation

_____ Reaction to conflict

WHEN FINISHED, GO TO PAGE __40__ TO COMPLETE THIS UNIT.

13.   ROTATING CENTERS

G+   L

READ FOCUS: Effects of the indispensable man. Effects of limiting channels of interaction. Sharing of responsibilities within the problem-solving group.

DO ACTIVITY: Select a coordinator. Divide into five-member groups and cluster chairs as diagrammed below: Present the same problem (arithmetic, puzzle or other "insight" problem) to all groups.

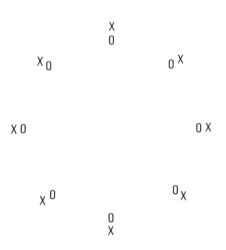

FIGURE 2.   Group Arrangements

Each group must work to achieve complete agreement on the answer to the given problem. In each group members in positions B, C, D, and E may communicate by leaning over and whispering to member A only. A may talk to all other group members at once, so he may talk aloud. An option to whispering is passing notes, but notes are more time-consuming. Start now.

COORDINATOR ONLY: GO TO PAGE __40__ RIGHT NOW.

14.   INTERACTION POKER

G   S

READ FOCUS: Effects of unbalanced contributions within the small group.

DO ACTIVITY: In a group of from five to eight members, discuss a decision-making problem of importance to the group or a controversial issue on which the group is evenly divided. Before you begin, select an "enforcer" from outside the group. The enforcer distributes fifteen poker chips (or tokens) to two group members, eight chips to two members, and two chips apiece to the remaining members. The enforcer will make a noise to suspend all interaction when any infraction of the following interaction rules occurs. The infraction must be corrected before group interaction may resume.

1. No one may talk without first throwing a chip in the container in the middle of the group.
2. Each chip entitles a member to one sentence.
3. Enforcer will penalize any violator one chip per violation or, for the violator without any chips remaining, expel the violator from the group. Discuss for twenty minutes.

WHEN FINISHED, GO TO PAGE   41   TO COMPLETE THIS UNIT.

15.   RECIPROCAL CRITIC GROUPS

G+   L

READ FOCUS: Group cohesion and solidarity. In-group and out-group identifications.

DO ACTIVITY: Divide fifteen to thirty members at random into three groups designated "Group 1," "Group 2," and "Group 3."

Group 1 Instructions: Get into a tight circle and draft a congressional bill that is designed to improve the quality of our national government. Work toward agreement and a first-draft version of your bill. You have fifteen minutes. Begin.

Group 2 Instructions: Ring yourselves around the Group 1 members in a larger, looser circle and observe the *content* of the discussion and the direction they seem to be going. Observe in a critical fashion and be ready to improve upon their bill, taking whatever notes will be helpful in this regard. Do *not* participate with Group 1 members in any way. You may confer quietly with other Group 2 members in a manner that does not disturb Group 1's discussion and work.

Group 3 Instructions: You are observers of the other two groups, so station yourselves in pairs as unobtrusively as you can and observe the *process* of both

groups. Look especially at group trends and developments as the exercise un-
folds. Stop Group 1 after fifteen minutes. Form Group 2 into a tight circle for
a discussion of the same problem and station Group 1 members in a loose ring
around them so they can observe Group 2's discussion. Stop Group 2 after ten
minutes and quickly reassemble both groups in the original pattern with Group
1 discussing and Group 2 observing. Stop Group 1 after five minutes. Assemble
your Group 3 in a tight circle in the middle of the room and discuss your observations loudly enough for all to hear. Stop after about ten minutes.

WHEN FINISHED, GO TO PAGE __42__ TO COMPLETE THIS UNIT.

16. DOUBLING

G+   S

READ FOCUS: Effect of group size on interpersonal communication processes.

DO ACTIVITY: Pick a partner.

1. Discuss a film you like for two minutes and stop.
2. Join the adjacent pair. Discuss for four minutes and stop.
3. Merge with the nearest four-member group. Discuss for eight minutes and stop.
4. Merge with an eight-man group. Discuss for sixteen minutes and stop.

DO ANALYSIS: Privately, fill out your responses to the questions below. When
everyone has finished, discuss your answers.

A. What, in detail, were the effects of group size on the structure of
interaction, on contribution rates, atmosphere, member perceptions and
attitudes?

B. What is the ideal size group? "Ideal" for *what*? Why?

END

17.   RANK DIFFERENCES₂

G   S

READ FOCUS: Individual differences within the small group. Effects of differences on group structure.

[There are certain dimensions along which people are often quite different
from one another. Some of these differences can be especially important in
influencing for better or worse the nature of a group experience, including task
achievement, interpersonal relationships, and individual adjustment within the
group. In this exercise we ask two questions: How do these factors improve
and retard group work? How can knowledge of these effects be used to the
advantage of the whole group?]

DO ACTIVITY: Privately identify five individual differences that you feel are
most important in making your group what it is at this point. Write them
below and rank them from "1" to "5" in order of importance, 1 being "most
influential."

Differences in:

Rank

_____   ____

_____   ____

_____   ____

_____   ____

_____   ____

DO ANALYSIS: Form into your group and compare your items and rankings. Note similarities and differences. Discuss the agreements and indicate the effects, both good and bad, of these influences on *your* group. Now, identify similar dimensions ranked differently by the members. Try to discover the reasons for these different perceptions.

END

18.   SEQUENTIAL SUBGROUPING

G+   S

READ FOCUS: Contrasting positions in group controversy. Perceiving similarities and differences in verbalized attitudes.

DO ACTIVITY: Start with a group of from fifteen to about thirty people. Discuss the best solutions to the energy shortage. Opinions and attitudes should be solicited for three or four minutes until two opposing views have been expressed that seem to split the group. Immediately divide into two subgroups by asking participants to join the subgroup representing the opinion closer to their own. Continue the critical discussion in the two subgroups for ten minutes. Stop and divide again, forming two smaller subgroups on the basis of attitude similarity. Continue to subgroup on the first indication of a basis for within-group differences, forming smaller and smaller groups. Follow this procedure until units of no more than two or three members exist.

DO FEEDBACK: Recall the several bases for each division. Note also any ways in which member behavior, including your own, changed from the initial to the final groups. Could you make any distinctions between your final position and that of those who ended up in your last group? How have you changed in your perception of group members' attitudes toward the topic through these successive discussions? Discuss.

END

D

Verbal
and
Nonverbal
Codes

19.   FRONT-TO-BACK DYADS

$$D \qquad G+ \qquad S$$

READ FOCUS: Need for feedback. Importance of eye contact and nonverbal cues. Integrated character of spoken and nonverbal signs.

DO ACTIVITY: Pair off with someone you do not know very well. Move your chairs close together at some distance from other pairs and face them in one direction in engine-caboose fashion. The person in front ("Front") should seek a comfortable position with eyes and head facing forward. Front is to remain silent until instructed otherwise—silent in speech and "silent" with body. Front is to refrain from any bodily movement that might convey any meaning—thoughts or feelings—to the person behind ("Communicator"). Communicators may have to lean forward and speak softly in Front's ear to overcome noise interference during the course of this exercise.

Communicator Instructions: Your first task is quite challenging, and you have only five minutes in which to perform it. Take a minute to think of some physical object that you treasure dearly—not for its extrinsic value, like money or precious gems, but for its deep emotional meaning to you in a positive sense. Perhaps this object represents a person, time, place, or event. Perhaps it is at home in a dresser or in your purse or billfold. Once you have selected something, identify that object for the person in front. Disclose what it is. Your goal is to communicate to your partner the nature of your *feelings* about that object as completely and as graphically as you can. With all of the expertise at your command, try to communicate fully your attachment to that object—what it means to you. Start now and stop in four minutes.

Following the same instructions, pick a current controversial topic about which you have strong feelings. Think about your feelings and ideas on that issue for a minute. Where do you stand? Your second task is to explain to your partner what your position is and why, so that Front will have some insight into your position. You have three minutes, so use it all. Begin.

(*Optional*: If you have enough time, you may reverse positions or turn chairs in the other direction at this point and repeat both tasks with a new Front and a new Communicator. If you do, be sure that Communicator selects a different controversial issue on the second task.)

Front may now turn around and discuss the controversial topic with Communicator for five minutes. Stop and begin analysis.

DO ANALYSIS: We have momentarily separated spoken and nonverbal communicative behavior. In this artificial situation a number of points concerning interpersonal communication are highlighted. Conduct an open discussion in class, reporting your feelings and what you noticed about yourself and about your partner in both the Front and the Communicator positions. What feelings did you have as Front? What about the need for feedback in face-to-face communication? What other functions does the face of the person with whom you are interacting serve with respect to your attempts at communication with that person?

END

20.   THE MUSIC OR THE LYRICS
A   D   G   S

READ FOCUS: Individual sensitivity to verbal and nonverbal signs.

[Although some scholars are currently looking at the question, there is no certainty about who among us is most capable of "reading" the nonverbal cues of others. Some psychotherapists have concentrated on such reading in order to diagnose the problems of their clients. At any rate, large individual differences probably exist among people in their abilities to attach valid meaning to the nonverbal signs given by other human beings. To a certain extent we all read these cues. But some of us are more verbally oriented and quite insensitive to much of the nonverbal behavior of others. Let us attempt in a crude way to assess our own relative orientations to verbal and nonverbal signs. We may obtain some insight into our own sensitivities and insensitivities in the process.]

DO ACTIVITY: Score each of the following six items by checking one of the two boxes provided:

1. In songs that I like the best, the thing that stands out more in my mind is the □music, □lyrics.

2. I probably talk to myself aloud □more, □less than others talk to themselves on the average.

3. In a jail cell for one year with nothing else to do, I would rather have a supply of □picture puzzles, □crossword puzzles.

4. In a brief, one-shot encounter with a like-sexed stranger, the dominant impressions of that person that I carry away come from the □stranger's words, □stranger's actions.

5. Compared with others that I know, the learning of an unfamiliar foreign language is (would be) □easy, □difficult for me.

6. When describing to a friend an incident that happened to me, I rely more on □telling, □showing (relating, demonstrating).

WHEN FINISHED, GO TO PAGE __43__ TO COMPLETE THIS UNIT

21.   REACTIVE SYMBOLS

G   S

READ FOCUS: Language and the visceral response.

DO ACTIVITY: Say each of the words or phrases below aloud so others can hear you.

COMMUNIST	NIXON	GOD
JESUS FREAK	FORD	MAKING LOVE
WAR	KENNEDY	MY FATHER

Select the *one* word or phrase that evokes the *strongest* emotional response or feeling in you as you say it or hear it said. Write it down and, without explaining the reasons, describe in writing the nature of your feelings at the time you experienced them—for example, love, hate, embarrassment, exhilaration, disgust, self-consciousness, and so forth.

WHEN FINISHED, GO TO PAGE __43__ TO COMPLETE THIS UNIT.

22. NONSENSE INSERT

SA   G   S

READ FOCUS: Communication of emotional meaning. Connotation, Vocal inflection.

DO ACTIVITY: Privately, select a public figure about whom you feel very strongly: a politician, novelist, scientist, entertainer. Write a brief paragraph conveying your feelings about this person such that the statement conveys the intensity of your feelings. Read this statement to your group in a manner that conveys your feelings. Give the group your written statement.

Group Instructions: Go over the statement and identify those expressions that were presented with the greatest emotional intensity by the author. Rewrite the statement, replacing only those words or phrases with nonsense words like "frimmish," "thickle," "spordcloist," "mathithmeputh," and the like. Return the statement to the author.

Author Instructions: Take half a minute to work out pronunciations of the nonsense words. Read the statement back, doing your best to mimic the intensity and inflection of your first reading.

DO FEEDBACK: Discuss the relation of connotative meaning and vocal inflection (paralinguistics). What did the nonsense words do to the reading? Words come to have a "life of their own," so heavily laden are they with subjective meaning. This is inevitable, but it also reduces the chance of communication occurring when feelings are extremely strong and where subjective meanings of communicators are incompatible.

END

1. YOUR OWN WORLD (Cont.)

DO ACTIVITY: Across the top of the paper, print seven column headings as follows: Age, Occupation, Income, Socio-economic Level, Race, Religion/ Creed, Politics. As accurately as you can, fill in the columns for each friend. If the person is not yet fully responsible for his or her own livelihood, estimate income of parents or supporting party under Income. When done, study how similar or different from you and from one another your friends are.

READ APPLICATION: These friends provide a lot of the data through which you understand and evaluate your experience—through which you see the world. You share things with them, and they, you. Are all your friends comfortably similar to yourself? To what extent are they of different races, religions, and political beliefs? Social classes? Our values, attitudes, and predispositions are more secure, less likely to be tested, in the comforting presence of those who are very much like ourself. The cost for this comfort, of course, is very high. We deprive ourselves of knowledge of the infinite variation in our world of people, thereby stunting our personal growth and perhaps even losing a healthy skepticism about some of our own most cherished values and opinions. We probably spend too much time with those who agree with us and too little time with those who don't—those who could add another dimension of understanding and information to our perspective. Following the lead of Willy S., that great Elizabethan social psychologist, we are *all* Horatios whose philosophies are unimaginably narrow.

DO ANALYSIS: React in a general discussion or small group to your own and to others' patterns of friends and to the above paragraph. What does all of this have to do with our attempts at interpersonal communication?

END

4.   FOR KEEPS (Cont.)

READ APPLICATION: Answer these questions in your own mind: What proportion of my change did I give away? How much did I receive? More or less than what I gave? Did I give to more than one? What method of distribution did I use? Equal amounts? To whom did I give? Why didn't I give to someone else? What was I thinking about during the distribution? when I saw what I received?

We might have used any other kind of tokens for this exercise, but money and what it represents is very important in our society. It is likely that everyone behaved in a way unique in some respect from everybody else. If you feel you acted just on the basis of convenience, why is it that others did not operate in this way?

DO ANALYSIS: The topic is individual differences. In groups of four to six, discuss what important and unimportant individual differences existed within your group with regard to thought and behavior during the exercise. Draw a list of five statements or generalizations concerning individual differences that can be identified from this exercise.

(*Optional*: Report these statements to the class and compare them with those made in other groups.)

END

6. FRONT-TO-FRONT DYADS (Cont.)

READ APPLICATION: Human beings are evaluating, judging, inferring creatures. We make so many judgments about what others are like—so many assumptions. We feel so certain we have the other "pegged." Yet we never get the opportunity to test our inferences and find out if we are right or wrong. On the other hand, we do tend to resent it when others "pigeonhole" us—as though we are more complex than anyone else. This exercise gives us a chance to check some of these inferences we make about others and to peek at the processes we go through in drawing them.

DO ANALYSIS: Conduct a large group discussion on impressions and the bases for what you wrote. Who made changes after interaction? Give some examples of changes and discuss why they were made. What impact do our silent evaluations have on our communication experiences with others?

END

7. IDENTITY DRAW (Cont.)

READ APPLICATION: Someone once said that there are at least four "selves" for every person: what I think I am; what you think I am; what I think you think I am; what you think I think I am. One writer terms "what I think I am" as one's "direct identity" and "what I think you think I am" as one's "meta-identity." To what extent one's meta-identity forms one's direct identity is still an open question. Yet what you think others feel about you does have a great deal of influence on your self-image and your behavior. Let us test your meta-identity by obtaining information from others about what they really think you are. In this way you can discover at least some things about how closely your perceptions of yourself match what others think about you.

DO ANALYSIS: In your project groups, pool your slips of paper with all the others so that no one can identify the authors. Have any group member draw one slip out of a container, number it, and read it aloud. Using the Personal Identity Sheet provided below, write down the slip number and the three attributes. Do this for all slips. Now, privately match each group member with the set of attributes that you most identify with that member's outward characteristics. This should be what *you* think that member is, *not necessarily* what you think the member really wrote. Identify each member in this way. Do not discuss your matchings until everybody is finished. Finally, reveal the results of your matching and assess how well your meta-identity matched others' actual perspectives of yourself. Discuss.

PERSONAL IDENTITY SHEET

Descriptions   *Member Name*

1. _____   _____

2. _____   _____

3. _____   _____

4. _____   _____

5. _____   _____

6. _____   _____

7. _____   _____

END

8. FANTASY DIALOGUE (Cont.)

DO FEEDBACK: Open to your fantasy notes. Trade notes with your partner. Discuss one another's fantasies. Compare your fantasized dialogues with what you really talked about and discuss the disparity between the two. How well did you predict the tone and feel of the actual dialogue in your fantasy? Discuss the role of expectations in communication behavior among strangers.

Among friends. What is the potential of fantasy as a method for anticipating difficult or important encounters? As a device for communication training in general?

END

9.   ROTATING DYADS (Cont.)

READ APPLICATION: Very quickly, you get a sense of how unlike a public speech interpersonal communication really is. Free interaction produces a rapid-fire cycle of perceptions and reactions from both parties that, as a unit, is unique and, at the start, largely unpredictable. Each comment or gesture is partly a "choice" by the communicator and partly a spontaneous and uncontrolled reaction to the behavior of the other. One key to effective interpersonal communication is recognition of this interconnectedness and of the exercise of judgment in adapting to the other person.

DO ANALYSIS: Below is an "Adaptation Analysis" form. Complete it privately. Afterward, conduct a discussion analyzing the cycle of action and reaction in communication and the relationship of this cycle to communicative goals. For example, how does this cycle expedite and promote and how does it inhibit and retard effective goal-oriented communication?

Adaptation Analysis

Directions: Circle one response category for each question

1. In the above exercise my thoughts were centered more on my own comfort and convenience than on that of my partners'.
   - (a) absolutely not
   - (b) don't think so
   - (c) think so
   - (d) definitely
2. With respect to the differences in the manner and characteristics of my partners, I can recall:
   - (a) nothing
   - (b) very little
   - (c) a number of points
   - (d) a great deal

3. I felt very comfortable with some partners and very uncomfortable with others.
   (a) Yes
   (b) No, only uncomfortable
   (c) No, only comfortable
4. (a) In general, I usually forge ahead and others adapt to me.
   (b) In general, I usually adapt to others to about the same degree that they adapt to me.
   (c) In general, I always seem to be adapting to others.
   (d) In general, I am not even aware of how much attention I pay to the uniquenesses of the person with whom I am communicating.

END

12. RANK DIFFERENCES₁ (Cont.)

READ APPLICATION: Form into your group. Compare rankings for a few minutes. Taking each dimension at a time, discuss frankly how the behavior of other members along that dimension has been noticed and thought about by you. Discuss how each dimension has influenced the way in which you have thought about and evaluated other members.

DO ANALYSIS: What dimension has caused more misinterpretations, misconceptions, and communication problems than the others? See if you can reach a consensus answer to this question. What can be done about it?

END

13. ROTATING CENTERS (Cont.)

Coordinator: After about five minutes of interaction, rotate all A members at once into the A position in the adjoining group, moving in clockwise (or some such) fashion around the room. Prohibit talking except according to the interaction rules, and let the groups continue to work on the problem. After about five minutes, rotate the A members again. If extra people are available, substitute them into the A positions. Work through four or five such substitutions for the central position in each group. When the first group reaches complete agreement on a correct solution or if time is short, before that point, stop the discussions. Instruct all to read the following "Read Application":

READ APPLICATION: We have manipulated artificially here what frequently occurs naturally in small group work. We have created the indispensable man by curtailing the interaction structure of the group. We have done it with rules instead of the usual forces of power, status, and personality and the usual differences among members in information that typically result in the same rigidification of group structure in "real life" groups.

In addition to limiting the group's efficiency and reducing the opportunity for creative interchange and interstimulation among group members, such rigid structures often lead to the creation of an *indispensable man* and the group's subsequent dependency upon him. When such a member is removed from the group, much group effectiveness is reduced through loss of information, organization, leadership motivation, and so forth. Also, members who are marginal contributors tend to feel even less involved and responsible for the task outcome. In a very few minutes we have tried to artificially simulate some of the processes and attitudes that in real groups develop over a longer period of time.

DO ANALYSIS: Discuss member reactions during the interaction on the problem. Discuss attitudes toward incoming "leaders." Did any groups start to "train" the incoming members after several disruptions? To what extent did your group adopt or evolve a method as it progressed? Solicit reactions of A people—what they thought about and felt about different groups during this experience. Identify three generalizations concerning the interaction structure and the sharing of responsibility in the small work group. Write them down here:

1.

2.

3.

Do you need to qualify these statements to achieve accuracy?

END

14. INTERACTION POKER (Cont.)

READ APPLICATION: This exercise should demonstrate the relationship of attitude and perceived opportunity to interact. Although some members will be quite happy to listen and let others do most of the talking, the perception of reduced opportunity to participate usually creates feelings of ill will toward the group project or toward members who are too talkative. Also, this unit should demonstrate a slowing down of interaction. Members are likely to give more thoughtful consideration before uttering their remarks.

DO ANALYSIS: Discuss reactions, especially the feelings of members during interaction. Restricted members who wish may now address the topic for a *short* period of time. What implications do these feelings and reactions have? How do most discussions proceed? What consideration is given in most discussions to the "undertalkers" who can not "get in"? Are members often restricted in participation in their group? How? What form do these restrictions take?

END

15.   RECIPROCAL CRITIC GROUPS (Cont.)

DO ACTIVITY: *Group 3:* Invite responses from Groups 1 and 2.

READ APPLICATION: This exercise was an attempt to illustrate quickly and artificially the emotional definition of a small group, a "we feeling," an identification of in-group versus out-group, a polarity. It is not unlikely, notwithstanding the brevity of the exercise, that some members began to get a feeling of solidarity and cohesiveness within their groups—despite certain disagreements that may have arisen. This aspect of the definition of a small group is difficult to put into words. It is hard to note the precise moment when members cross the line between being a loose collection of individuals and become a group. But that is probably unimportant. What is important is that once such strong (or even weak) group identifications are formed, your behavior as a member is much more dependent on your group, on its structure and process, and on the norms and values that emerge from its structure and process *irrespective* of whether you know it or not or like it or not.

DO ANALYSIS: Individually, identify in writing any norms of procedure that developed and any forms or symbols that came to represent *in your mind* any one of the three groups during the exercise.

END

20.   THE MUSIC OR THE LYRICS? (Cont.)

SCORING: Score a "1" for each check of any of the following: "lyrics," "more," "crossword puzzles," "stranger's words," "easy," and "telling." Mark a "0" for each item with the alternative response. Add the six items. A total of 0 or 1 *may* indicate that you are more nonverbally oriented; a total of 5 or 6 *may* mean that you are more verbally oriented.

DO ANALYSIS: Compare yourself with someone who responded quite differently as indicated by the discrepancy in total scores. These questions are not really a "test" of orientation. They are offered here to set you thinking about how your own awareness and lack of awareness operate to influence your responsiveness to the signs emitted by those around you. Compare and discuss. Do you have any different evidence concerning your orientation?

END

21.   REACTIVE SYMBOLS (Cont.)

READ APPLICATION: These reactions are what we mean by "connotative" meanings. Some words call up associations beyond the literal dictionary definitions. Because *meaning* resides in the language user and not in the language itself, the reaction to any one such symbol varies greatly from one user or listener to another. Regardless of how justified or unjustified the reactions of others seem to you, the associations that have evolved in all of us are powerful forces that can be used to improve or retard effective communication, to move or restrain us from action.

DO ANALYSIS: In your group compare reactions, intensities of reaction, and explanations for the reaction. Can you really completely "explain" your most intense reactions in a rational way? Listen carefully to others and try to understand their feelings surrounding these symbols. When finished, see if the group can draw conclusions about (1) how to *overcome* barriers to interpersonal communication that connotative associations entail, and (2) how connotative associations can be used to *facilitate* interpersonal communication. Report results.

END

II

Methods for Studying Interpersonal Communication

A

Simple Observation

23.   OBSERVER-REPORTER₁

A   D   E

READ FOCUS: A technique for observing and reporting on group communication by designating an "Observer-Reporter" (OR).

[An OR is not only a valuable instrument for letting the group know *how* it is doing and *what* it is doing, an OR is also a useful source of information and insight into communication within small groups, both one's own and other groups.

Before proceeding further, we need to define certain terms and describe certain functions and roles of the OR that will be referred to in this unit and throughout this section.

1. *Definitions.*   The following two definitions pertain to interaction between people:

Interaction Content: The specific verbal statements group members make on or off the topic of the group task. Nonverbal behavior can also comprise group content for the observer interested in that aspect.

Interaction Process: Patterns of behavior within the group without regard to the particular ideas or other specific *content* of the interaction.

For example, it would be a feature of group *process* that two members never contribute to the general discussion, but talk only with one another. However, what they say specifically to one another would be a matter of *content.* Here are sample quotations from an observer's report:

Content: "Frank said 'Forget it' and was quiet from that point on."
Process: "After one member's withdrawal from participation, several other members who were previously silent entered fully into the discussion."
Content: "Tom's idea of staffing day-care centers was greeted positively by four members and negatively by the other three. Terry said she thought it was utterly impractical, and then Ziggy argued that you could not condemn it before it was given a trial run."
Process: "The group reacted to one idea for thirty minutes, divided into two camps, and never initiated an original idea from that point on."

It should be clear by now that interaction *process* is an abstraction or "liftout" from interaction content and consists of the patterns of behavior at the whole-group level. On the other hand, a complete or partial recounting of interaction *content* would consist of nothing more than a set of "minutes" of the verbal exchanges within the group from the first moment to the last.

2. *Functions.*   The functions of the OR are twofold: (1) to observe the interaction *process* (not content) of the group, and (2) to report back to the group on these observations. This means that the OR usually takes notes during his observation period, organizes them prior to the end of the discussion, and reports back immediately at the end. Novice OR's will gain from working with a partner or two and pooling their observations prior to report time, even if the partners are also novices.

3. *Role.*   The OR is either a group member who steps outside of the group temporarily to perform the observations or an outside-of-group person who has had or wants to acquire experience in facilitating task groups. During observation the OR does *not* interact at any level with the group and is positioned physically beyond its perimeter, enabling him to maintain the necessary psychological "distance" from group content. The OR's role is to help the group improve itself—not to improve the group himself, singlehandedly. The OR plays a "reminder" role, helping the group become aware of interactional processes. In most groups members are usually too busy with the task at hand to deal with this facet of interaction.

4. *Observing.*   In verbal interaction we usually pay attention to details of what is being said—the content—at a particular moment. But the OR must not be drawn in or he will do a poor job of identifying group processes.

So much happens so fast in the small group that any attempt to "get it all" results in nothing of value. Therefore, the OR must begin his observation period with some instrument(s) to guide or limit his attention to specific aspects of group process. Samples of such instruments may be found throughout this section and at the end of Unit 23. The ideal is for the OR to become sensitive enough to the needs of his group and skilled enough at observation that he can tailor his own instrument for guiding his observations in a particular group or situation or at a particular time. Such instruments typically do two things: (1) classify aspects of group process, and (2) count interactions within each class.

5. *Reporting.* In the report back to the group, the OR may give one of three kinds of reports. He may describe, he may describe and interpret, or he may describe, interpret, and evaluate.

Descriptive Reporting: The OR reports his observations of group process; does not go beyond the patterns of behavior she saw and heard.

Interpretative Reporting: The OR describes *plus* reports inferences he has drawn about *why* it happened the way it did.

Evaluative Reporting: The OR reports and interprets *plus* makes suggestions to the group on how they might improve their interaction processes. This reporting can include suggested procedures, special methods, or just bringing some difficulty to the attention of group members.

The manner of reporting should be informal with the OR physically moving into the group. He should report as a peer, avoiding harsh criticisms of individuals and avoiding any superiority in manner.]

DO ACTIVITY: Using Observation Forms A, B, and C (page 51-55), become an OR for groups in which you are a member. For the same or different groups, collect observations in the manner indicated and complete all forms. Subsequent to each observation, complete an Observer Report Form (page 57) and give your report orally to the group(s) you have observed.

Submit a brief statement of any problems you encountered in reporting back to your group(s). Suggest solutions for each problem encountered. Hand in this material to your group along with your observation forms.

OBSERVATION FORM A

Aspect: Frequency of contribution by comment of each group member.
Method: Five samples of 2 minutes of discussion during 20-minute interaction period

Member's Name	Record Sample 1	Record Sample 2	Record Sample 3	Record Sample 4	Record Sample 5	Totals
1.						
2.						
3.						
4.						
5.						
6.						
7.						
8.						
9.						
10.						

OBSERVATION FORM B

Aspect: Frequency of contribution by main speaker in a 20-second interval.
Method: 30 samples of 20-second intervals, scored once every 40 seconds.

Member's Name   *Tallies of 20-second intervals**   *Totals*

1. _____ | — | — | — | — | — | — | — | — | — | — | _____
2. _____ | — | — | — | — | — | — | — | — | — | — | _____
3. _____ | — | — | — | — | — | — | — | — | — | — | _____
4. _____ | — | — | — | — | — | — | — | — | — | — | _____
5. _____ | — | — | — | — | — | — | — | — | — | — | _____
6. _____ | — | — | — | — | — | — | — | — | — | — | _____
7. _____ | — | — | — | — | — | — | — | — | — | — | _____
8. _____ | — | — | — | — | — | — | — | — | — | — | _____
9. _____ | — | — | — | — | — | — | — | — | — | — | _____
10. _____ | — | — | — | — | — | — | — | — | — | — | _____

*Keep a record of the 30 samples by crossing out a number each time one is completed:
1 2 3 4 5 6 7 8 9 10 11 12 13 14 15 16 17 18 19 20 21 22 23 24 25 26 27 28 29 30

OBSERVATION FORM C

Aspect: Frequency of fact, opinion, and suggestion in group discussion.
Method: Two 5-minute samples within a 20-minute discussion. Classify members'
statements. Do not count short agree or disagree words like "Yes" and "No."
Do not count questions. Record by crossing out one number per occurrence in
the appropriate category.

First 5 Minutes:

Fact: 1 2 3 4 5 6 7 8 9 10 11 12 13 14 15 16 17 18 19 20 21 22 23 24 25

Opinion: 1 2 3 4 5 6 7 8 9 10 11 12 13 14 15 16 17 18 19 20 21 22 23 24 25

Suggestion: 1 2 3 4 5 6 7 8 9 10 11 12 13 14 15 16 17 18 19 20 21 22 23 24 25

Second 5 Minutes:

Fact: 1 2 3 4 5 6 7 8 9 10 11 12 13 14 15 16 17 18 19 20 21 22 23 24 25

Opinion: 1 2 3 4 5 6 7 8 9 10 11 12 13 14 15 16 17 18 19 20 21 22 23 24 25

Suggestion: 1 2 3 4 5 6 7 8 9 10 11 12 13 14 15 16 17 18 19 20 21 22 23 24 25

Totals

Fact: _____

Opinion: _____

Suggestion: _____

OBSERVER REPORT FORM

Aspects Observed:

1.

2.

3.

4.

5.

Descriptions of Group Process:

Interpretations of Group Process:

Evaluations and Suggestions:

24. OBSERVER-REPORTER$_2$

A   D   E

READ FOCUS: More practice on observing and reporting skills.

DO ACTIVITY: Be an OR for a group in which you are *not* a member and whose proceedings are unfamiliar to you. Before you commit yourself, be sure that this group operates as a small group and not in the parliamentary mode. Be sure to refrain from participation during observation. Make your own guiding instruments from the list of ideas below or elsewhere. Use the Observer Report Form provided here to write a report following your observations. On a separate sheet (page 63) indicate what level of feedback seemed appropriate to this group: Description? Interpretation? Suggestions? How was it received? What are your ideas for doing a better job with a different group next time around?

Ideas for Observation Report Forms

Who-to-whom patterns

Initiating ideas versus reacting to others' ideas

What happens to ideas: Added to? Modified? Abandoned? Applied? Related? Used?

Task-relevant comments versus task-irrelevant comments

Agreeing comments versus disagreeing comments

OBSERVER REPORT

Aspects Observed:

1.

2.

3.

4.

5.

Descriptions of Group Process:

Interpretations of Group Process:

Evaluations and Suggestions:

OR PROBLEMS

Observing:

Reporting:

25.   INTRODUCTION TO ROLE PERSPECTIVE: ANALYSIS₁

SA   D   E

READ FOCUS: Studying and identifying member roles in small groups.
[We have referred to interaction *content* as the "what" of interaction and interaction *process* as the "how" of interaction. Group *structure* is the product of the interaction process. Among its results are power-status hierarchies, specialization of member roles and functions, the communication network, a sociometric pattern, and developed norms and rules. Group process refers to the workings of a group; group structure refers to the various outcomes of those workings. And coming full circle, group structures, once formed, guide subsequent group processes. The aspect of group structure that we will focus on here is that of the members' *roles.* We will wish to identify the *behavioral consistencies* of specific group members where they exist within one small group discussion or from one discussion to another. These behavioral constants we will call "roles."

Sometimes an analysis of the behavior of a given group member reveals a pattern to his contributions—a pattern made of a number of repeated elements. This pattern when described and understood can be called his role in that group. A role does not encompass all of the member's behavior, but it does describe a limited number of the more enduring and more constant aspects of his communicative (and noncommunicative) behavior.

Each of the example behaviors below could be an element in a role of a group member. These are examples *only*; they are provided as a starting point for the role analysis we will do here.]

Some Examples of Role Elements

Makes references to personal experiences***gets off the subject***interprets the discussion questions***interrupts others***summarizes and pulls discussion together***keeps track of time***gets things started*** praises, encourages, or otherwise "supports" other members***jokes and makes humorous remarks***makes peace***challenges others' opinions ***arbitrates differences of opinion*** argues technicalities***tries to get people to contribute.]

DO ACTIVITY: With a Behavior Profile form (pages 67-69) in front of you and working with a partner, pick two or three group members and tally the number of behaviors they exhibit in each of the example categories. *Ignore* all other behaviors except the elements listed here. Toward the end of the discussion, retire to the side with your partner and write a profile of elements (role description) for each person observed. Compare the resulting profiles.

DO FEEDBACK: Report back to the group on your observations and on whether each target member was observed to have a definitive role or not. Give observed individuals a chance to question and respond. This discussion should be conducted in a spirit of inquiry and not of judgment. If you had to do it over again, which elements would you include in your analysis that you did not include this time? Which ones would you drop?

END

BEHAVIOR PROFILE

Directions: Shade one square for each observation of a particular element

Elements of Behavior

Member's Name: _____

Makes references to personal experiences												
Interprets the discussion questions												
Summarizes, integrates contributions												
Gets things started												
Jokes and makes humorous remarks												
Challenges others' opinions												
Argues technicalities												
Contributes factual information												
Gets off subject												
Interrupts others												
Keeps track of the time												
Praises, encourages, "supports" others												
Makes deadlock-breaking suggestions												
Arbitrates differences of opinion												
Tries to get people to contribute												

Elements

Member's Name: _____

Makes references to personal experiences

Interprets the discussion question

Summarizes, integrates contributions

Gets things started

Jokes and makes humorous remarks

Challenges others' opinions

Argues technicalities

Contributes factual information

Gets off subject

Interrupts others

Keeps track of the time

Praises, encourages, "supports" others

Makes deadlock-breaking suggestions

Arbitrates differences of opinion

Tries to get people to contribute

26.   ROLE ANALYSIS$_2$

A   D   G   S

READ FOCUS: Identifying roles in the small group without the aid of example
role elements.

[The role analysis conducted in the preceding unit should enable you to
identify roles within a small group without the aid of the example role elements.]

DO ACTIVITY: Working either alone or with a partner, observe a group of
which you are not a member. Do *not* interact in the group. Select a manage-
able number of group members (two or three) who are actively participating
in the discussion. Take the first five or ten minutes to get an idea of how you
could describe or classify for tabulation some of the contributions that they
make. Then, using the Behavior Profile form below, perform your role analysis for each target individual along the lines of the elements of behavior you
have selected. Note that some behavior may overlap from member to member
and some may not. When you are done, make an assessment on whether there
is an overall pattern for any of the observed. Check with partner and prepare
a brief report.

DO FEEDBACK: Report to the group or, if not appropriate, to the observed
members only, carefully noting which of the elements were repeated often
enough to justify their inclusion in a role description. Notice also what particular combination of elements makes up each individual's role as observed.
Lead the group in a discussion exploring the relation of these roles to group
interaction and task achievement.

END

BEHAVIOR PROFILE

Direction: Shade one square for each observation of a given element.

Member's Name: _____

Elements of Behavior

1.

2.

3.

4.

5.

6.

7.

8.

9.

10.

27.   TREND ANALYSIS

D   L

READ FOCUS: A trend analysis of group content or processes.

[One way in which to understand behavior in dyads or in small groups is to obtain a panoramic view of interaction content and process characteristics— that is, a view of the dyad or whole group across a substantial period of time. To do this, it will be helpful to find a group that will be pursuing the same task on three or more separate occasions. A longer-term observation can provide insights into the developmental nature of interaction that a fragmented or "one-shot" observation does not provide.]

DO ACTIVITY: With a partner, preselect categories of observation; for example: agree or disagree statements; task or nontask behaviors; group animation level (indexed by volume and frequency of interruptions); magnitude of silences; "I" and "we" references. Isolate behavioral elements you feel may be significant or useful to know. After you have selected your categories of observation, decide on a method of scoring and sampling (e.g., observation of every other sixty-second time period). Now, on the Trend Analysis Record provided on page 77, identify in writing your selected variables, your categories of behavior, and method of scoring categories or category definitions, and your sampling system.

DO FEEDBACK: Tally categories, compare with partner, and prepare a brief commentary describing the results. Present this information to the observed parties, inviting analysis and criticism.

END

TREND ANALYSIS RECORD

Identify selected variable(s):

1.

2.

3.

4.

Describe behavior categories and method of scoring for each variable:

1.

2.

3.

4.

Describe sampling method:

In the space below, set up your Data Collection Form on which you will record your observations for each selected variable.

28.   INITIATION AND REACTION

A   S

READ FOCUS: Effects of initiation and reaction contributions on group interaction.

[Utterances of *initiation* are those that *introduce* an idea, opinion, fact,
suggestion into the group discussion. These are contributions that initiate ideas
or, by offering something new to the idea of another member, add to the
originality of the discussion. *Reactive* contributions are *responses* to something someone else in the group has said. Reactions can be made to other reactions as well as to initiations. Examples of reactive contributions are clarification, elaboration, and repetition of ideas already introduced into the discussion. Arguments that focus exclusively on another's idea and present little
new information are also reactions. Both initiation and reaction contributions
are necessary for productive group interaction.]

DO ACTIVITY: As an OR of your small group, note the name of each participant on the Observation Record provided below. For each continuous contribution by any member, classify that comment as either "reaction," "initiation," or "combination." Unless initiation and reaction are equally balanced
in the member's comment, score it according to the dominant thrust of the
comment, thereby using the "combination" category as seldom as possible. At
the beginning of the discussion, listen carefully for awhile in order to get the
"feel" of the categories.

DO FEEDBACK: After you have completed a profile on these characteristics for
every member of your group over a period of time, report the ratio scores for
each individual and for the group. Explain to the group what you have done
and initiate a discussion on what the group's pattern of ratios might imply for
improving group effectiveness.

END

OBSERVATION RECORD

Member Name	Initiation	Reaction	Combination	Individual Initiation/Reaction Ratios	Group Ratio
1.				/	
2.				/	
3.				/	
4.				/	
5.				/	
6.				/	
7.				/	
8.				/	
	Total ___	Total ___	Total ___		/
1.				/	
2.				/	
3.				/	
4.				/	
5.				/	
6.				/	
7.				/	
8.				/	
	Total ___	Total ___	Total ___		/

81

29.   EXPRESSING AND COMMUNICATING

A   D   E

READ FOCUS: Self-expression in communication.

[Self-expression and communication are definitely not the same thing. Effective interpersonal communication usually relies on self-expression *plus* something else. Communication entails self-expression, but self-expression does not necessarily achieve communication. A would-be communicator may engage in self-expression. Self-expression may make that person feel better. It may relieve his tension and even result in the communication of something to a listener—especially if that listener knows the person rather well. But most of our efforts at communication involve those who do not know us intimately. Here, communication involves adapting to the other person, coding one's ideas and feelings so the other person may better interpret them—a reaching out to the other person in repeated attempts to elicit meaning and understanding. This reaching out process is necessary when communication, not mere self-expression, is the goal. Precision in language, sensitivity to the attitudes of the other, and background information may all be essential requirements in the effective communication of a message.]

DO ACTIVITY AND ANALYSIS: Identify three instances in which self-expression failed to achieve communication. Using the Expression-Message Form below, briefly describe the expressive utterance and, if possible, the meaning that was intended but not received. Discuss these with a friend, analyzing the misunderstandings therein.

END

EXPRESSION-MESSAGE FORM

Self-Expression

(what was said or done with little
or no consideration of or adaptation to the listener)

1.

2.

3.

Probable Message

1.

2.

3.

30. MESSAGES WITHIN MESSAGES

A   D   E

READ FOCUS: Modification of verbal messages through the use of secondary messages.
[Communicators are not always content to just express thoughts and let it go at that. Occasionally, we feel the need to modify our verbal expressions even as we present them. That is, we often insert *secondary* messages within a primary message in an attempt to smooth our encounters. One investigator has identified six classes of secondary messages, which he terms "communication tactics."[1]

CLASSES OF SECONDARY MESSAGES

Tactic	*Examples*
1. Pre-interpretation:	"You probably won't agree with this, but—"
	"Listen, you'll like this—"
2. Post-interpretation:	"You're probably mad because of what I said—"
	"Now, you are probably leaping to conclusions—"
3. Pre-apology:	"Maybe I should not say this, but—"
	"I haven't thought this through yet, but—"
4. Depersonalized Motive Revelation:	"No reflection on your mother, but—"
5. Altruistic Motive Revelation	"Because we're friends, I will tell you—"
6. Identity Confirmation:	"Having gone through your problem, I can tell you—"

The first three types of secondary messages are self-explanatory. The motive revelations (Tactics 4 and 5) come in two forms. In the depersonalized form the speaker reveals that his motive for commenting is objective and disassociated from any negative reactions that the comment might bring about. He thereby shucks responsibility for the comment. In the altruistic form, the speaker reveals that his motive is his special concern and sense of responsibility toward the other. In both cases the motive revelation implies to the listener that he or she should not "hold it against" the speaker. The identity confirmation (Tactic 6) is meant to establish credentials or special insights, entitling the speaker to make the comment he makes. Name-dropping, for example, is a form of identity confirmation familiar to all of us.]

[1] Eugene A. Weinstein, "Toward a Theory of Interpersonal Tactics," in *Problems in Social Psychology*, ed. Carl Backman and Paul Secord (New York: McGraw-Hill, 1966), pp. 394-97.

DO ACTIVITY AND ANALYSIS: Note different occasions on which you use several of these messages-within-messages and try to analyze what you were trying to achieve. More often than not, we employ these devices automatically, so ingrained are they in our verbal utterance. Did your qualifying messages accomplish what you wanted them to? Why or why not? Identify a friend or acquaintance who overuses one or another of these tactics—someone who uses them as a matter of course, and therefore ineffectively. Discuss the possible reasons why someone you know overuses these tactics.

END

31.   CONFLICTING COMMUNICATION CODES

A   D   E

READ FOCUS: Conflicting verbal and nonverbal messages.

[When a person says one thing while his nonverbal behavior conveys a message that conflicts with the words, we invariably trust the nonverbal message more than the verbal. To put it another way, we automatically tend to disbelieve the verbal and give the nonverbal priority. We all have heard someone say "I couldn't care less" in such an impassioned manner that we *know* the person really cares a great deal. "I love you" can be said with a look and a tone that really means "I hate you," and vice versa.]

DO ACTIVITY: Over the next week, keep a diary of instances in which what is said is refuted by nonverbal cues. Describe carefully the circumstances and the effects of each instance until you have compiled a record of three such instances in which others convey conflicting communications—and three in which you monitored yourself doing it.

DO ANALYSIS: Discuss your notes with a partner or a friend and consider how such mixed messages can (1) aid and (2) impede effective communication. Discuss when such mixing of signals is intentional and when the communicator is completely unaware of the contradiction. In other words, when did the speaker mean to do it and when did the nonverbal part just slip out, belying the utterance. Identify a public figure who does this frequently and discuss the effect this conflicting behavior has on you.

END

32.   COMMUNICATION OF EMOTIONS

G+   L

READ FOCUS: Accuracy and inaccuracy of our inferences from nonverbal responses of others. (As one of several pairs of observer-reporters, you need a one-way observation mirror for this exercise.)

DO ACTIVITY: Give a five- or six-member group a particularly difficult and challenging task. Ask them, for example, to agree on features of an ideal education system. Seat members so each can be seen from the observer room behind the one-way mirror. Keep the sound turned off in the observer room. Start the group working on its task. Then, working in OR pairs in the observer room, identify the expressions of an emotional state by viewing the "silent" interaction through the observation window. Use the emotional states listed in the Observation Record below as a guide, but note also any other emotion that you think is occurring in one or more individuals. Fill out the Observation Record, indicating the emotion inferred and why you inferred it. After fifteen or twenty minutes, turn up the sound and listen for ten minutes.

DO ANALYSIS: Reconvene with the group. Observer pairs should report what they have written. Invite discussion and corrective responses from the group members. In your interaction be sure to consider these questions:

1. When were you wrong and when were you accurate in your inferences? How were you misled by silent language?
2. How often do we probably misinterpret the other's internal state even when we can hear what the other is saying?
3. Are we more prone to such misinterpretations at some times than at others? When?

END

OBSERVATION RECORD

Emotion Inferred	*Person*	*Specific Basis of Inference*
Hostility		
Agreement-Enthusiasm		
Authoritativeness		
Tension		
Boredom		
Uncertainty		
Puzzlement		
Hope		
Disgust		
Appreciation		
Futility		
Bitchiness		
Ridicule		
Pleasure		
Apprehension		
_____		
_____		
_____		
_____		
_____		
_____		
_____		
_____		
_____		
_____		

33.   GROUP MINICULTURE

G   L

READ FOCUS: The reward system in group interaction.

[This unit requires that the group as a whole agrees to enter into a frank and open discussion of its reward system. The discussion is to center on the following questions: Who gets rewarded in the group relative to other group members? What do members get rewarded for—that is, on what basis are members rewarded? What form do the rewards take? What rewards would each member prefer?]

DO ACTIVITY: 1. Discuss fully all the above questions. Probe every lead regarding the source of rewards in this group, how they are dispensed, why they are distributed in the way they are. Do roles and functions of members, the power distribution within the group, or the group's decision-making processes have anything to do with the group's reward system?

2. If you have not already covered the following points, discuss what is rewarding to each individual member, what is punishing to each member, who feels good about where they fit into the group, who feels on the very "edge" of the group.

DO ANALYSIS: Assess what aspects of the group's reward system revealed here promote growth and excellence and what aspects produce inhibition and mediocrity. In other words, taken as a whole, how does the existing reward system make some members productive and others counterproductive? And still others apathetic? Isolate aspects of the system that should be changed, invent ways to change them, and implement these changes.

DO FEEDBACK: At a later group session, check to see if your change measures took hold. If they did, evaluate the results; if they did not, find other means to improve your reward system. Report any useful or important outcomes to other task groups.

END

B

Active
Intervention

34.   NORM BREAKING

A   D   G   E

READ FOCUS: Norms for behavior in interpersonal communication settings,
their functions and effects.

[At times a good way to explore some of the protocols and manners in
human exchange is to challenge them momentarily. In this unit we will inten-
tionally break a norm governing the way in which things are usually done in a
given interpersonal space—such as an office, a corridor, a classroom, a public
meeting, a post office, a bank, a supermarket, a bus stop. Note: The potential
value of this exercise resides in a careful analysis and discussion of the observations gathered during the norm breaking and not in the mere act of counter-
norm behavior itself.]

DO ACTIVITY AND ANALYSIS: 1. Identify a norm of behavior governing
face-to-face communication in some public place—some pattern of behavior,
in other words, that seems to be an assumed and accepted mode. Some examples might be hushed tones in a bank or supermarket, averting the eyes of
another in a public passenger vehicle, waiting passively for the instructor to
initiate daily activities in a classroom. 2. Break the norm in a manner that is
not self-conscious. Break it confidently and without appearing to be trying
to shock or disturb those in the immediate vicinity and, of course, without

breaking the law. 3. Observe carefully the verbal and nonverbal reactions of others. Look for clues that could help you explain or understand either the reasons for that norm or its functions. Some functions might be rather obvious, others will not be. For example, why the hushed respectful lowering of the voice in the bank? Are banks really twentieth-century temples? 4. Write down the results of your observations, carefully reconstructing the situation into which you intruded, the way in which you did it, and the reactions you engendered.

DO FEEDBACK: At a convenient time report your venture to someone and discuss the importance or unimportance that such a norm may have for effective encounters within that setting. Elicit others' ideas on this subject.

END

35.   THE NONVERBAL DANCE

A   D   G   E

READ FOCUS: Coordination among the various nonverbal facets of behavior; some effects.

[Since antiquity, novelists and playwrights have employed the nonverbal orchestrations of fictional characters in their writing. Recent years have seen an upsurge of interest in nonverbal behavior and nonverbal communication on the part of behavioral scientists. Many of these behaviors, taken largely for granted before, may be found to contain important sources of information about the people who exhibit them. For example, two investigators several years ago presented evidence supporting their hypothesis regarding the relationship of nonverbal behavior to the level of intimacy of communicators.[2] Extrapolating from this work, we propose that the amount of eye contact, the amount of smiling, and the proximity of two communicators reflect their level of intimacy. Converting this observation to more tangible terms we have: The amount of eye contact (in seconds), combined with the amount of smiling (in seconds), and the average proximity (measured in face-to-face distance) may give an estimation of the intimacy level (comfortable level) of two communicators. The relationship might be crudely abbreviated as follows: Intimacy = EC $\times$ Sm $\times$ 1/Prox. To paraphrase, during a fixed period of interaction the more freqeunt EC and Sm and the less Prox between the two, the more intimate the two are likely to perceive themselves to be. Couples in love exhibit

[2] Michael Argyle and James Dean, "Eye Contact, Distance, and Affiliation," *Sociometry*, 28 (1965), pp. 289-304.

the most intimate levels of the three variables. Conversely, strangers exhibit the lowest levels. We can all think of exceptions to this index. During or after a fight, for example, sullen mates may stay their distance; strangers, on the other hand, may on occasion "groove" rather quickly. Still, in general the intimacy index suggested above probably holds some validity for the large majority of our encounters.]

DO ACTIVITY: This activity can be done with a partner, both of you taking turns observing the other's "experiments" with a stranger from a "safe" distance. The object is to develop a sensitivity to how we unconsciously and consciously manipulate three nonverbal variables—eye contact, smiles, proximity— to maintain a comfortable level of intimacy with another person and how each adapts to the behavior of the other from moment to moment using the same three variables. Suppose, for example, that a stranger of five minutes leans close to you, looks into your eyes, and utters a remark in a subject area usually reserved for your more intimate friends and associates. How would you react? Most likely you would either move back, avoid some of the gaze, refrain from smiling, or some combination of these reactions. Suppose too, that in interacting with a close friend, you notice that the friend has been avoiding your eyes, smiling less than usual, or talking from farther away than usual. Would you not immediately sense that something is wrong? Experiment with these three factors alone and in combination as described below, noting the reaction of others. How does another manage to return the intimacy level to the usual and comfortable level by varying these same factors? Do both (1) and (2) below:

1. Violate the comfort level of a person you do not know very well through greater eye contact, more smiling, or closer position during interaction. Note your own reaction as well as that of the other.

2. Violate the comfort level in the other direction with a close friend (less EC, less smiling, greater distance). Do this exercise with persons of both sex.

DO ANALYSIS: Discuss with your observer-partner how the others reacted. Discuss any conclusions you have about the communicative impact of these spontaneous, out-of-awareness nonverbal "dances" in which we all take part.

END

36.   BLIND TALK

D   G   S

READ FOCUS: Some effects of visual perception of nonverbal behavior on group processes.

[It only takes a few minutes to discover what effects—bad and good—the visual perception of nonverbal behavior has on group processes. Early in your group's life, before interaction patterns and member roles are established, is a good time to do this exercise. One method of studying the effect of "eyeball" interaction on group functioning is to dispense with it entirely and contrast the resulting group processes with the usual manner of group functioning.]

DO ACTIVITY: You need to cover your eyes for this unit. Group participants are to put blindfolds (scarves, etc.) over their eyes and continue their current discussion project for at least ten or fifteen minutes. By prearrangement, someone outside the group should indicate when ten minutes have elapsed. Begin. On the signal remove the blindfolds and go to the "Do Analysis" step.

DO ANALYSIS: Discuss the following aspects of this experience:

1. Was the vocal intonation more noticeable with the blindfolds on? Why or why not?
2. Were feelings and thoughts of members during interaction any different from the discussion when members were visible?
3. What are the values and the difficulties that visual data pose to the group's best functioning?
4. Here are three typical errors in interpreting the meaning of what others are saying that occur regularly in most small groups. What role does nonverbal communication play in each?
    (a) Members read more evaluative meaning into the contributions of the speaker than is intended by the speaker.
    (b) Members distort contributions on the basis of past contributions by the speaker.
    (c) Members overrely on a single source of information in the group.
5. How can negative effects of visual data be checked when the eyes are not artificially covered as in this exercise?

END

37.   STRANGE ENCOUNTER

D   E

READ FOCUS: Heightened awareness of specific behavior during interpersonal interaction.

DO ACTIVITY: In a public setting, locate a stranger who is alone. While your partner observes unobtrusively, approach the stranger and strike up a conversation. Do this in a way that does not define the situation for the stranger— that is, do *not* approach with any specific purpose like asking for the time or for directions. You may have to try this several times before you are able to engage a person in small talk. When you do, sustain the conversation for a few minutes and retire to some place where you can immediately record in writing: (1) your impressions of the stranger's behavior, (2) your impressions of the stranger's feelings; (3) your own behavior and feelings during interaction.

Reflect back on the encounter and write down any observations that you can recall in the above areas. Perform this unit four times—twice each with strangers of both sexes. Take turns with your partner in the observer role. Discuss these observations and compare them with your partner's observations of yourself and the strangers.

WHEN FINISHED, GO TO PAGE _123_ TO COMPLETE THIS UNIT.

C

Instrumented Feedback

38.   POST-MEETING REACTION SHEETS₁

SA   G   L

READ FOCUS: Use of the Post-Meeting Reaction Sheet (PMRS) for group feedback.

   [Information on PMRS's (see below) comes from the combined perceptions
of the group members themselves. The sheets may take many different forms,
limited only by the author's imagination. Here, we present several typical
PMRS's and discuss their various uses. There are a few guidelines to keep in
mind that will be helpful to you:

1. *Anonymity.* More information and greater accuracy may result if respondent
   anonymity is preserved and if respondents are apprised of this fact.
2. *Clarity of directions and items.* An advantage of the PMRS is that it takes
   only a few minutes to fill out and tabulate. However, this advantage is for-
   feited if directions are carelessly written or ambiguous and if the significance
   of the items on the sheet is poorly conveyed. In this event respondents may
   not be replying to the same thing, in which case the information obtained is
   inaccurate or useless.
3. *Brevity and simplicity of items and scales.* Another advantage of the reaction
   sheet is that the information it contains can be quickly tallied on the spot

and reported back to group members for immediate analysis and discussion. This feature can be lost if items have been inexpertly written or instruments for measurement have not been carefully developed. Limit the PMRS to no more than four or five judgments (items).

A final note on ambiguity: Ambiguity in *written directions* on the sheet wastes everybody's time. What is clear to a writer is often confusing to the user. Therefore, prior to using PMRS's, check the directions, item wording, and the measures with another person to detect errors or problems. Of course, in certain instances ambiguity in the wording of a particular item may be acceptable, depending on the kind of information the writer (or group) wishes to elicit. An item for identifying a group's attitudes toward its "leadership," for example, would necessarily have to be vague in certain language if the purpose is to find out how the respondents themselves define and relate to leadership. In such a case, use of the elegantly vague term "leadership" would be entirely appropriate.]

DO ACTIVITY: Distribute the PMRS's below to your group members and ask them to respond to all items on each PMRS. When all have finished, turn back to this page for the "Do Analysis" step.

DO ANALYSIS: 1. Privately, compare the variations in methods of scoring PMRS items: circled numbers, circled adjectives, slashed lines, ranking, and so forth. Other methods are possible depending on what you want to find out. A reaction sheet could contain only a single item, if that information is all you need. Sample Sheets A and B contain one kind of item scored in the same way. Samples C and D contain a mix of items. Note that some rating scales have an ideal position in the middle of the scale with negative extremes at both ends. Other items are unidirectional and the "size" of the rated quality corresponds to the numerical points on the rating form.

2. Tally member responses for each item on all sheets and complete the data summary sections of each.

3. Evaluate each PMRS with your group and extract any information that you can from them. Look first for patterns. Note the spread of scores on the different items. What could that mean? Continue analysis and discuss how to improve some of the sample items for your particular group.

END

POST-MEETING REACTION SHEET A

Directions: Slash (/) the horizontal line at the point that represents your reaction to the question in each item.

1. What is the nature of our leadership?

Too Centralized	Just Right	Too Diffused

2. How satisfied am I with the group's progress?

Completely Satisfied	Not Sure	Completely Dissatisfied

3. How pleased am I with my own part in the group process?

Yuk	Ho-Hum	Whoopee

4. To what extent have we been tapping all of our group's resources?

Great Extent	Somewhat	Not at All

(To summarize group's responses, superimpose all marks onto a single sheet.)

POST-MEETING REACTION SHEET B

Directions: Rank all group members except yourself from "1" to "6" where "1" is the highest rank and "6" is the lowest on each of the below qualities.

	Member Name	*Rank*	*Totals*

1. Objectivity of contributions:

2. Sensitivity to others:

3. Value of information given:

4. Value of thinking:

5. Acceptance of responsibility for the group's task:

Data Summary: Compute a simple sum of ranks for each member in each of the five categories by totaling ranks from all respondents. Place totals in column. If some members have used tied ranks (Note Bill and Joe in Example 1), convert them in this way:

Example 1:	Bill	1	1.5	Example 2:	Seth	1	1
	Joe	1	1.5		Lucy	2	3
	Pete	2	3		Chris	2	3
	Sal	3	4		Ziggy	2	3
	Wanda	4	5		Zelda	3	5

POST-MEETING REACTION SHEET C

Directions: Circle the responses that most closely represent your feelings.

1. The extent of my contributions in *other* groups in general is:

1	2	3	4	5	6	7	8	9	10
Very Low				Average					Very High

2. The most difficult problems that plague our group arise because we seem to be (choose *one*):

Dominated–Distracted–Uncommitted–Belittled–Blocked–Uncertain-Uninvolved–Uninformed

3. Other members probably feel that the part I play in this group is:

−5	−4	−3	−2	−1	0	1	2	3	4	5
Too Marginal					Just Right					Too Central

(Data Summary: To see the pattern of scores, transpose all responses onto one sheet for each item. Then compute averages for items 1 and 3. Item 1 Ave. _____ Item 3 Ave. _____

Tabulate the frequency of "mentions" for each description in Item 2.)

POST-MEETING REACTION SHEET D

Directions: All items are self-explanatory.

1. The *one* thing we most need to do to improve our group's effectiveness is:

    _____ Create special roles to facilitate our efficiency.

    _____ Select tasks that everybody is *wild about.*

    _____ Appoint temporary "leader-expeditors" for each new task.

    _____ Get rid of a particular member.

    _____ Experiment with several new group methods.

2. In our group we are hampered most by our failure to:
    (rank "1" through "6" where "1" is the most serious lack in member
    contribution).

    _____ Initiate

    _____ Clarify

    _____ Question

    _____ Analyze

    _____ Encourage

    _____ Listen

    (Data Summary: Sum the frequency of "mentions" in Item 1. Convert
    tied rankings in Item 2 and sum rank scores for each choice.)

39.   POST-MEETING REACTION SHEET$_2$

G   S

READ FOCUS: Interpretation of the Post-Meeting Reaction Sheet items.

DO ACTIVITY: Below are two sample data summaries from PMRS items, followed by some questions. Study the items and the data summaries, and answer all of the questions in writing. Do this individually, and refrain from commenting until everybody in your group is finished.

SAMPLE DATA SUMMARY 1

What is the nature of our group procedures?

GROUP A:	✓✓ 3	2	1	✓ 0	1	✓ 2	✓✓ 3
	Too Chaotic			Just Right			Too Rigid

GROUP B:	✓✓ 3	✓✓✓ 2	✓ 1	0	1	2	3
	Too Chaotic			Just Right			Too Rigid

GROUP C:	✓ 3	2	✓ 1	✓ 0	✓ 1	2	✓ 3
	Too Chaotic			Just Right			Too Rigid

1. What does the difference in spread for Group A mean? For Group C?

2. What kind of information does Sample B give you? Compare all three samples. What different interpretations can you validly make about each? Based on these data, for which group or groups would you feel a recom-

mendation is justified? What kind of recommendations, if any, would seem warranted?

SAMPLE DATA SUMMARY$_2$

How much satisfaction do you get from your participation in this group?

						√	√		√	√√	√
GROUP D:	1	2	3	4	5	6	7	8	9	10
	None									a Great Deal

To what extent do you think this group is effective in achieving its goals?

		√√	√	√				√		√
GROUP D:	1	2	3	4	5	6	7	8	9	10
	None at All									Great Extent

3. What might this mean and what recommendations or suggestions might be made to Group D from this information?

DO ANALYSIS: After all members have completed answers to the three questions, discuss your answers and any differences in interpretations. Obviously, there is a danger of overinterpreting these data sheets, or "reading in" more than is justified. There is also a danger of missing important clues about the group's process that could be helpful to the group and that could have been uncovered by a more careful and probing analysis. List below any statements

of interpretation that your group agrees are justified and that might be useful
to that mythical group from which the data came.

1.

2.

3.

4.

5.

6.

7.

END

40.   POST MEETING REACTION SHEETS₃

A   L

READ FOCUS: Development of a focused PMRS.

[Often no existing PMRS can elicit the information needed by a group
that can match the power of an instrument developed by an individual group
member. Any member can help a group by taking some initiative and creating
items for a PMRS and then administering it to the group. Beforehand, the
member needs to be aware of the problems inherent in directions, item wording, item scoring, and interpretation. The first three of these problems were
discussed in the "Focus" portion of Unit 38 and the fourth was the subject
of Unit 39.]

DO ACTIVITY: Devise a PMRS of several items to obtain useful information
about member feelings, member attitudes, and group methods. Prepare it by
using the practice sheet on page 113. Check with someone outside the
group to correct and polish it. Duplicate several copies and after a group
session, administer the copies to group members. Tabulate the results and lead
a discussion about them. Explain why you included the items you did. At-

tempt to draw inferences. Make any recommendations to your group that are warranted by your observations. Finally, evaluate the PMRS instrument. Did it elicit the information you wanted? Should it be modified? Why? How? Make your PMRS—its intent, level of success, and suggested modifications—available to other groups.

END

DRAFT PMRS

Directions:

Data Summary:

41.   ABSTRACTED FEEDBACK

SA   D   G   E

READ FOCUS: A method for studying dyadic and small group processes.

[Sometimes issues, ideas, personalities, and emotions present such an intricate onslaught of stimuli to students of interpersonal communication, that it is hard to sort out the trends and undercurrents going on in rapid-fire, face-to-face encounters. For a better understanding of these trends and undercurrents, abstracted feedback[3] can help us sort out the ramblings in these exchanges. It can be especially useful for a group grappling with difficult decisions and where interaction involves subject matters and exchanges that are emotionally charged.]

DO ACTIVITY: It is very difficult for someone who has been intensely involved in a discussion, or who has strong feelings about a particular subject, to prepare an abstracted feedback sheet. So get a partner and, together, listen carefully to a discussion taking place in a small group, but do not participate in the discussion. Jot down portions of statements being made that seem to represent the main points of contention and disagreement. Try to identify several points of view. After the discussion use these notes to write a dialogue with a cast of characters labeled "A" through "K." A cast of six could represent a discussion by twenty people; a cast of three or four could represent a group of six to ten members. The point here is that the characters in your "play" do not have to represent *specific* members of the group on a one-to-one basis because each character's "lines" should form a composite of bits and pieces of ideas and arguments made by the various real characters in the group. In writing the script keep the lines relatively short and fast-paced. But keep them as true to the actual discussion as possible. The entire script should fit on one page. Then replace all central ideas, arguments, and viewpoints or solutions with numbers (or lower-case letters).

Goal: You are trying to capture the emotional tone and climate of the group discussion; you are not trying to write a literal account of what was actually said. You can borrow certain words and phrases from the original to convey the moods and intensities of the interaction—as long as such phrases were used by more than one person. Study the sample abstracted feedback sheet below:

SAMPLE ABSTRACTED FEEDBACK SHEET

Directions: Describe the major underlying problems in the following abstraction from one of your discussions and suggest the probable solutions to those problems.

[3] T. G. Grove, "Abstracted Feedback in Teaching Discussion," *The Speech Teacher,* 16 (March 1967), pp. 103-8.

A: Everytime we make a decision, we change it and waste more time making the same decision...facing the same problem all over again. It's very frustrating.

B: That's how I feel. That's why we should leave things the way they are.

C: How can you leave things the way they are when nobody likes the way they are? I'm as tired of this hassle as the rest of you, but we have no choice in the matter. The decision must be made so that we can move on to other things.

A: I never said I wanted to leave things the way they are. I do want to adopt a new proposal as long as we have to change it again, but C's right—we need to come to some agreement right now.

D: But we talked this all over before and decided. Who's to say that we won't change all over again...that somebody won't find something wrong with this plan and start the damn mess all over again. I have other things I could be doing, you know, and I know a goodly number of others here who feel the same way.

E: What about F and G? They haven't said one word yet. I'd like to know how they feel.

C: I would too. I mean, this affects them as much as anyone, and yet they've not helped very much with this problem. (*To F and G.*) Just what do you say?

F: There's not really too much to say that hasn't already been said. I go along with A, C, and the rest of you. I do think something should be done today about this, so we can forget about it.

C: Well, most of us seem to be in agreement, then. So let's move on to decide. Plan Z is very good because of the advantages p, q, and r. I say we adopt it.

A: "r" is not really an advantage, because it means different people will not be evaluated the same way. I'd rather adopt Plan Y because of features s and t.

D: All right, since we've got to decide, I want to say that t is certainly an advantage, but if Plan Y means s applies to everybody, I can't go along, because I think s has nothing to do with the purpose of this project.

F: "s" is very necessary to consider if we're going to get the most possible out of this project.

C: We can't get into a long drawn-out discussion of s at this point. It seems to me that s is entirely irrelevant and we have to consider the other factors now, so let's talk about the advantages and disadvantages of X versus Y.

A: But we've been doing that for 30 minutes. I'm in here to learn about W. Let's take a vote right now.

B: This is ridiculous. We spent 75 whole minutes on this simple issue two weeks ago and now here we go again. We spent all that time and everybody had a chance to talk, so why bother just so someone can change it again? At this point I couldn't care less....

This abstracted feedback sheet is not a literal plagiarism of the original discussion on which it is based. Everything is paraphrased. Note that this one page is sufficient to illustrate recurring problems of a group of 24 members discussing an issue for approximately fifty minutes. Yet it depersonalizes individuals. It does not point a blaming finger at one or a few members.

In working on your own script, just listen carefully for the underlying difficulties in the interaction. Use imagination to depersonalize your abstraction.

Note in this sample how some issues were raised and never followed up, how others were mixed together and confused. Note how the group made a show of soliciting ideas from quiet members, but did not wait to hear from all of them. Also, isn't it obvious that this group needed to make an early decision on an acceptable method for legitimizing an emerging decision? In addition, much time and energy was spent at the "wailing wall," but without a useful analysis of what went wrong before and of how to assure that it will not happen again.

You are ready to begin. Remember, your goal is to cut through the smoke-screens of verbal complexity and emotional intensity—to reduce the discussion to a few important patterns that stand out in the group process. Begin.

DO FEEDBACK: As soon as possible after the target discussion, duplicate copies of your script and distribute it to the members. If you have done your job well, the group will recognize their discussion immediately. Lead a critique of the group processes using the script as a guide to improving the quality of future deliberations. Discuss.

END

D

Role Playing
and
Simulation

42.   PHYSICAL ANALOGUES

A   G   S

READ FOCUS: Physical analogues of a group's structural characteristics. Example: A sociometric pattern.

[Sociometric choice refers to a group process in which members select their relational preferences to certain others in the group. Their choice is made by positioning themselves in relation to another member (or members), a physical statement analogous to the way they feel toward the other person with respect to such specific dimensions as "who would you like to work with on a difficult assignment?" or "with whom would you most prefer to socialize?"]

DO ACTIVITY: 1. Select a "Focal Person" (FP); Move the furniture back out of the way, and tell the FP to stand in the center of the room and close his eyes.

2. Each group member is to stand close to or far from the FP, depending on how close that member feels to the FP.

3. Instruct the FP to open his eyes and note where members of the group are positioned in relation to him. This is how they feel. Note how they differ.

4. All of you look around at one another. Notice your distance to FP relative to other members. Are people you feel close to positioned about the same distance from the FP that you are? How about those you feel distant from? Are their distances to the FP similar or dissimilar from yours?

5. Instruct the FP to reposition members closer to or farther from him on the basis of his (FP's) feelings of distance from each. How many changes did he make.

6. Have the FP order members nearer or farther according to how he *expected* them to line up the first time. Compare this pattern with the second one. To the first one.

7. Look around at one another and see how you stand in relation to others as arranged by FP's expectations.

DO ACTIVITY: Suggest different physical analogues of other group phenomena that could shed some "light" on the structure of this group. Write it up and share it with other groups.

END

43. JOHN AND MARSHA

D   G   S

READ FOCUS: Introduction to paralinguistics (vocal characteristics) in the non-verbal communication of meaning.

[Paralinguistics includes those nonverbal facets of spoken language (vocal quality, pitch, volume, and rate of and changes in those facets) that supplement or dominate the verbal-language meaning of utterance. The exercise of this unit is simple—often comic—in effect. But it can be used to begin an analysis and understanding of the interdependency of paralinguistics with the verbal aspect of utterance.

You may remember or have heard about a popular record that received heavy play some two decades ago entitled "John and Marsha." The entire record consisted of a man and a woman uttering the other's name only, to wit: "John" and "Marsha." As a dialogue, "John" and "Marsha" is not very interesting, but the soap-opera manner in which each spoke the name of the other ranged across the gamut of emotional meanings, working up to and concentrating on innuendos of sexual intimacy. Some listeners were offended by this risqué quality. This is *not* our intention in this exercise.]

DO ACTIVITY: Pair off with a member of the opposite sex with whom you feel comfortable in friendly interaction. Slowly, in a matter-of-fact way, begin a John-Marsha dialogue using only those two words. Each in turn speak the "name" of the other once or several times and continue to do this for a number of turns. Try to convey in your utterances the largest range of meaning that you can convey in about five minutes of dialogue. Take your time at first to think about different ways to change your utterance and change it as soon as you have another "way." Actively experiment with the factors of vocal quality, rate, pitch, volume, and changes in these factors. (*Optional:* Conduct the exercise in the center of the room with the remainder of your group looking on.)

DO FEEDBACK: Discuss different effects of specific vocal characteristics. Discuss also the relation between other nonverbal facets of behavior: face, gesture, body, posture, and so forth.

END

44.   GROUP MIRRORING

SA   G   L

READ FOCUS: Other's perception of self through mirroring.

[Mirroring is a process whereby one communicator reflects the immediate verbal or nonverbal behavior back to the behaver. After a group has been together for some time and perhaps has encountered some difficulties, it may be useful for members to receive a "dose" of themselves so they can see how they are perceived by others. This activity should be done with a light spirit plus a willingness to learn from seeing oneself from the point of view of another group member.]

DO ACTIVITY: Get your group to agree to interrupt your current project for fifteen minutes. Each member take a minute to think about how he or she could role-play the member seated to his or her right. Each will try to portray the dominant impressions of that person's behavior in the group in the past, adopting aspects of his or her verbal and nonverbal manner. Now, continue your interrupted task, *but* in the role of the person to your right. Proceed until each member has had some chance to take part.

DO ANALYSIS: After fifteen minutes or so, stop. Discuss the role-played impressions that are shared by the rest of the group as representing the mirrored person—and those that are not. Identify any problems or implications for group harmony and efficiency and suggest solutions for each problem discussed.

END

E

Games

G   G+   S

READ FOCUS: Analysis of interaction structure.

DO ACTIVITY: In a group of six or less members, identify a policy question that is not only crucial to the future activities of your group but one that must be resolved *now*. Distribute forty or more chips equally to group members so that each member has between five and ten chips. Select an outside-of-group person to be the "House." House keeps time, activates the buzzer at the instant of illegal talking and until the "pot is right," and enforces these interaction rules:

1. A talker is legal only after he has bought talk time at a cost of one token for thirty seconds by putting the token into the container.
2. Time may be bought in whatever amount the talker foresees he will need without interruption. But, because no refunds will be given for unused time, buying in more than single units may result in wasted tokens.
3. Unused time at the end of a paid-up period can be used by a second talker *after* he has paid his token.
4. Interruptions of legal talkers costs three tokens plus one additional token for the first thirty seconds.

5. Tokens may not be loaned or given away. The only way to prevent the buzzer from sounding or to turn it off once it has started is to ante up.

Announce the policy question to be resolved again and begin now.
WHEN FINISHED, GO TO PAGE 123 TO COMPLETE THIS UNIT.

46.   TOKEN ANALYSIS₂

G+   L

READ FOCUS: Member roles and group resources.

[After group members work together for a while, they come to expect certain behavior from one another. In this exercise, the group, starting with a difficult task and a limitation on total number of member contributions, must decide how to allocate its time before beginning work on the task. The rules for this unit are the same as those for Token Analysis₁:

Select an outside-of-group person to be the "House." House keeps time, activates the buzzer at the instant of illegal talking and until the "pot is right," and enforces the interaction rules below.

1. A talker is legal only after he has bought talk time at a cost of one token for thirty seconds by putting a token into the container.
2. Time may be bought in whatever amount the talker foresees he will need without interruption. But, because no refunds will be given for unused time, buying in more than single units may result in wasted tokens.
3. Unused time at the end of a paid-up period can be used by a second talker *after* he has paid his token.
4. Interruptions of legal talkers costs three tokens plus one additional token for the first thirty seconds.
5. Tokens may not be loaned or given away. The only way to prevent the buzzer from sounding or to turn it off once it has started is to ante up.]

DO ACTIVITY: You have thirty minutes and fifty tokens to use in that time. See how much progress you can make on your group's current task. However, prior to beginning this discussion the group must decide how it is going to distribute the tokens. It must distribute *all* the tokens, and members must put in writing a well-thought-out basis for their distribution *before* they are given out. The group may *not* rely on equal or on random distribution; the basis of distribution must be carefully considered. You have fifteen minutes to agree among yourselves on your distribution method, to put it in writing, and to effect the distribution of the tokens. Title your group report, "Basis for and Outcome of Our Token Distribution." Begin now. When finished with the report, work on your current group task for 30 minutes following the rules stated above and using the token distribution plan described in your report.

DO FEEDBACK: Read your group report to other groups. Discuss and solicit evaluations from others. Discuss with group members how your group could use its members more effectively.

END

37.   STRANGE ENCOUNTER (Cont.)

READ APPLICATION: We are so caught up in the business of communicating to achieve goals on the one hand and so involved in enjoying ourselves in casual or social communication on the other that we rarely take the care to observe the *process* of interpersonal communication. This exercise gives us a chance to notice some things about ourselves and about others regarding communicative behavior.

DO ANALYSIS: Discuss your reactions, your partner's, and those of the strangers. Do these have any implications for your communication effectiveness or ineffectiveness? Share your written observations with others to discover what similarities and differences were reported in the several strange encounters and what conclusions, if any, can legitimately be drawn from them.

END

45.   TOKEN ANALYSIS$_1$ (Cont.)

DO ANALYSIS: After the session is over, determine the relative cost (extent) of each member's participation by counting the remaining tokens. Discuss: Do these reserves tell you about how you use your member resources? To what extent did members contribute equally? Is it realistic to expect that on any given task, members will contribute equally? Do extreme differences in participation exist? If so, is this a sensible use of members? How do you account for the differences that do exist? Are they temporary or fairly representative of typical interaction within your group? Can you improve upon the quality of your interaction by reallocating member time differently from the usual pattern? The removal of which member would have most radically altered the pattern of contribution in this particular discussion? How would it alter it?

END

III

Approaches to Changing Communication Behavior

A

Change Games

47.　CIRCULAR SEQUENCE TAG₁

G　　　S

READ FOCUS: Listening; relating to the ideas of others.

[The language and perceptual habits within which we move are narrow and anticreative. They keep us from "seeing" the range of implications that a bright comment or a fresh idea might have. So, we sit back and react only to those images that are easy for us. Because we are so selective in our responses we don't really have to tax our imaginations in most group encounters. Also, we listen too passively much of the time, knowing that the chances are remote that we will ever be required to relate our ideas to those of some specific other person. This unit represents an attempt to break out of this mold by imposing a tight structure on a twenty-to-thirty-minute discussion.]

DO ACTIVITY: In a five-to-ten-member group, sit in a small circle. Follow these rules for interaction:

1.　The first talker is the tallest, and this person must begin the experiment by discussing any topic that he wishes to take up.

2.　The order of talking moves clockwise around the group. Each person to the left of the current talker must speak as soon as the current talker finishes.

There are no exceptions to this order, and everyone must talk in his own turn.

3.   Everyone must also follow the "tagging" rule—that is, each speaker must *immediately* tag his comments to something said by the previous speaker. Each talker must start with the words "With respect to...," relating what he wants to say in a *logical way* to something the previous speaker said. He should think of something that argues against, supports, or elaborates on a comment by the previous speaker, and then add his own comment on the same or another topic.

4.   The discussion is to move around the entire group twice, then reverse itself (move counterclockwise) for two cycles and stop.

DO ANALYSIS: Careful listeners typically do better in this exercise than those who are not as alert to implications of others' remarks. Discuss differences between active versus passive listening. Report your conclusion and unusual occurrences during the exercise.

END

48.   CIRCULAR SEQUENCE TAG$_2$

G   G+   S

READ FOCUS: Listening carefully; relating to the ideas of others; supporting others.

[Here we will use a circular sequence method to practice supporting others —finding something of value in their contributions.]

DO ACTIVITY: 1. Arrange your four-to-ten-member group in a tight circle.

2. You are the Award Committee for the "Most Valuable Human Being Alive" annual banquet and you must come to a consensus on a list of the three most deserving nominees, each of whom is reasonably well-known to all of you. Before beginning discussion, each of you jot down two potential nominees.

3. Throughout, only one member may talk at a time and you must find *some element* in the comments of the previous speaker that can be genuinely praised or approved *before* presenting your own ideas.

4. The discussion must move clockwise around the group twice and then twice more in a counterclockwise direction. Each member must talk in turn and must support—sincerely—some element in the previous speaker's remarks.

READ APPLICATION: Those who had the most trouble with this exercise may not be as good listeners as others. Some might rejoin that they are good listeners when they want to be. But it is precisely at those times when we do not take the trouble to listen that we miss important distinctions and ideas in our groups—displaying an insensitiveness that frequently leads to other interpersonal problems. In addition, relating to the ideas of others in productive ways can require considerable skill.

DO ANALYSIS: Discuss for five minutes any difficulties with this exercise. After that, finish your "nomination" task without the constraints upon interaction imposed to this point.

END

49.   COMMUNICATION CHALLENGE

G+   L

READ FOCUS: Practicing communication skills through role-playing difficult situations.

[One of the most effective ways in which to practice communication skills is to use role-playing in difficult situations with demanding individuals. All of us have had periodic one-on-one encounters in which our communicative goals are frustrated almost from the start because of the other's attitude toward our ideas or because of our own angry or frustrated reaction toward the other's behavior. In this exercise we will focus on the situation in which a difficulty arises because of the other person's dogmatic stance against some idea, proposal, or request that you have. Dogmatism has many sources, but it may stem from the other's general attitude, rank, longevity in position, or even seniority.

This exercise works best when participants share a common occupation or experience. Public-school teachers, for example, have often had the experience of trying to change a program that required the cooperation of colleagues. Construction workers have known how hard-nosed company foremen can be when it comes to eliminating an unsafe working condition. Most job applicants have faced the skeptical, difficult, or manipulative personnel director, and many students have had to confront a professor on the issue of a make-up test or a tardy term paper. Nurses, attorneys, law-enforcement officials—practically every vocational group—have their share of unpleasant stories involving difficulties in one-to-one communicative challenges.

Although the sharing of a common work experience is helpful in this unit, it is not an absolute prerequisite for obtaining value from it. We are going to do two things in this exercise: We are going to create a communicative challenge for another group, and we are going to try to meet a communicative challenge presented to us by another group.]

DO ACTIVITY: 1. In groups of four to six members select or create a one-on-one situation in which one person, the "Communicator," must use his persuasive powers on another person or enlist—against appreciable odds of success—the other person's cooperation. The other person is best described as "difficult." Fashion this situation after one that members of your group have experienced. Carefully and briefly describe in writing (a) the traits and title, office, or relationship of this "Difficult Person" (DP), (b) information concerning the history of the situation leading up to the encounter between the DP and the Communicator, and (c) the specific communicative goal that the Communicator will attempt to reach in interacting with the DP. Use the Communicative Challenge Sheets provided on pages 133 and 135.

2. Create a DP by integrating all of the worst traits and attitudes of difficult individuals encountered by your group into a single believable character. Give your DP a name and describe the traits and behavior of this "individual" on the sheet provided.

3. Make a copy of this Communicative Challenge Sheet and mark both sheets with a form of group identification. Hand the copy to the second group.

4. Select one person from your group that you think could most effectively role-play the DP created by your group. Feed this member ideas for use in encountering the Communicator from the other group. After your DP is so "armed," send him off to the side to study or practice his notes. Your DP's goal is to react realistically to the Communicator who will approach him.

5. While your DP is preparing his behavior, turn to the challenge sheet that you received from the other group. Read it, and select a second role player who might be able to "disarm" the DP described on that group's sheet. Feed this Communicator strategies that will help him to achieve the goal indicated on this challenge sheet.

6. Have the DP from your group sit behind a desk or in some position appropriate to his situation. The Communicator from the second group should then enter the scene and begin to work on his communicative goal. Both the DP and the Communicator should proceed to respond according to their "nature" and purpose. At some natural cutoff point, no more than ten minutes into the exchange, stop the dialogue.

DO ANALYSIS: 1. Role players should report their feelings and reactions to their roles, and explain why they reacted the way they did. Onlookers should join in the discussion. They are to consider how well the Communicator did, what approaches were taken, what was and was not effective, and what alternatives to the behavior witnessed could be used to advantage.

2. Proceed to the second challenge sheet and corresponding role players. Follow up with analyses and discussion. In your analysis, discuss the reciprocal and contingent characteristics inhering in one-to-one encounters and the

effects of these characteristics on the role players' behavior. Were you ever almost "forced" to react in a particular way because of what the other did or said in this exercise? Write a summary of the most important points or ideas that came from this exercise.

END

50.   TOKEN-STRUCTURED INTERACTION

G   L

READ FOCUS: Encouraging specific contributions by members of the small group.

[Often a group overlooks the kind of contribution that it needs to incorporate in order to do a good job on a decision-making task. In a sense this exercise attempts to familiarize members with a target communicative act: the asking of questions and the making of procedural suggestions. Different kinds of communicative acts can be encouraged in the same manner, depending on what members believe might help the group.]

DO ACTIVITY: 1. Select an outside-of-group person to be the "House." The House will then distribute five tokens to each member and instruct the group on the interaction rules. The House will assign a discussion on the current group task or any problem calling for group agreement.

2. House keeps time, activates the buzzer at the instant of illegal talking and until the "pot is right," and enforces all of the other rules.

3. A talker is legal when she or he has first bought talk time at a cost of one token for thirty seconds by putting the token into the container.

4. Time without interruption may be bought in whatever amount the talker foresees will be needed. But, because no refunds will be given for unused time, buying in more than single units may result in wasted tokens.

5. Unused time at the end of a paid-up period can be used by a second talker *after* he pays his token.

6. An interruption of legal talkers costs one token plus one additional token for the first thirty seconds of interruption and each thirty seconds thereafter.

7. Tokens may not be loaned or given away. The only way to prevent the buzzer from sounding or to turn it off once it has started is to ante up.

8. *Questions* to the group are *free* as long as they do not contain assertions or new information. All *procedural suggestions* (how the group should operate) are also *free*.

9. The House is to monitor the group discussion until the problem is solved, the group task is completed, or until no tokens remain in the group.

DO ANALYSIS: Assess the extent to which the free contributions were used. Could they have been used to even greater advantage—that is, more frequently? To what advantages can each of these two kinds of contributions be put? List the uses.

END

COMMUNICATIVE CHALLENGE SHEET

_____
Group

DESCRIPTION OF THE "DIFFICULT PERSON":

DESCRIPTION OF COMMUNICATOR'S GOAL:

OTHER FEATURES OF THE CHALLENGE SITUATION (Background of problem, etc.):

COMMUNICATIVE CHALLENGE SHEET

_____
Group

DESCRIPTION OF THE "DIFFICULT PERSON":

DESCRIPTION OF COMMUNICATOR'S GOAL:

OTHER FEATURES OF THE CHALLENGE SITUATION (Background of problem, etc.):

51.   ATTITUDINAL CHAIRS

G   L

READ FOCUS: Listening skills; understanding the position of others.

[Here we are going to develop sensitivity toward points of view different from our own and challenge our own listening skills at the same time.]

DO ACTIVITY: All group members are to fill out the ranking task below to represent their individual feelings on what our nation's research-expenditure priorities should be in the next decade. Rank "1" through "4" where 1 is the highest and 4 the lowest priority.

_____ Physical sciences

_____ Social sciences

_____ Biological sciences

_____ Humanities

Group members are then to identify their rankings and attempt to clarify their point of view, communicating their position with clarity and persuasive effect. They are also to make sure they understand what every other member's position is. After fifteen minutes, stop. If there is any group member whose feelings are still unknown or unclear, take two minutes and inquire into them now.

WHEN FINISHED, GO TO PAGE 159 TO COMPLETE THIS UNIT.

ß

Selected Communication Skills

52.   ATTITUDINAL ROLE REVERSAL

D   S

READ FOCUS: Listening skills; empathy for the position of others.

[In the appendix to his widely read novel, *1984*, George Orwell introduced "Goodthink"—a symbolic strategy of his totalitarian society—a society that had little patience with politically unacceptable points of view.[4] Here we will practice some "Badthink" to help us understand and relate to points of view that are different from our own.]

DO ACTIVITY: Quickly and privately, complete the questionnaire below, indicating your feelings on each issue. Circle the response that best represents your position. (See page 139.)

Pair off with a partner and locate the item containing your most dissimilar reactions. Argue about these issues. Do your utmost to convince one another of your own view and to reject the other's. Do everything you can think of to influence your partner, *but* be sure to listen carefully to your partner's comments during this process. Discuss for ten minutes.

WHEN FINISHED, GO TO PAGE <u>160</u> TO COMPLETE THIS UNIT.

[4] George Orwell, *1984*, (New York: New American Library of World Literature, 1961), p. 250.

1. Programs of mandatory birth control should be established on a worldwide basis.

   1   2   3   4   5   6   7
   Negative   Affirmative

2. The best hope of the world rests with

   1   2   3   4   5   6   7
   Certain   International
   Nations   Organizations

3. The political party that has best served the interests of the United States in my lifetime is the

   1   2   3   4   5   6   7
   Republican   Democratic

4. My attitude toward legalized gambling is

   1   2   3   4   5   6   7
   Favorable   Opposed

5. My position with regard to pornography laws is one of

   1   2   3   4   5   6   7
   Opposition   Support

53.   TAGGING AND RELATING

A   S

READ FOCUS: Balancing participation within the small group.

[We have all been in a group with excessively lopsided participation among the members—where some are talking all of the time and others little or not at all. The following exercises pertain to the difficult problem of changing the pattern of interaction for the purpose of (1) gaining the involvement of a low participator and of (2) dealing with the repressive effect of a verbal dominator.

For some group members, contributions are limited to single words of approval and disapproval or short phrases chanced only during moments of noisy chatter—and usually lost. When such brief comments can be heard, immediate reinforcement and acceptance may go a long way toward enticing the quiet member into more valuable and extended contributions.]

DO ACTIVITY: Here we will practice the art of *tagging* comments that are short—have little substance to them—or come from members who are usually not heard by the group. By "tagging," we mean perceiving and responding to such utterances in a way that gives the quiet member a gentle "push" into the active group. This encouragement can be registered by placing an idea or part of an idea with merit or potential in a context that makes it more attractive or meaningful to other group members. If the target member is perceived to be on the verge of making a contribution, his or her impulse to do so can be reinforced by adding to the idea and turning it back over to the originator. Practice can be achieved by experimenting with the weaker ideas of *any* group member. Experience indicates that the payoff of this form of communication may come in an increase in the quality and quantity of contributions from the heretofore quiet member. Try this experiment several times before evaluating its effects. It will take some practice to acquire the finesse needed to engage the person in question. But it is in the interest of any group member to make the effort. Group work may be enhanced in a variety of ways by the "new" member.

DO ACTIVITY: Develop a knack for *relating* an idea currently under consideration in the group to a comment or idea made earlier by the target individual. Relating does take a creative talent. Such verbal knitting together of two different streams of thought can be successfully combined with an "eyeball" invitation to the quiet member to elaborate on the related ideas. If in your attempts to make such connections clear to the group you inadvertently misrepresent the point of the target individual, he may be all the more ready to enter the discussion and set things straight.

DO ANALYSIS: After several thoughtful attempts at tagging and relating, assess the results, the problems you had, and describe both in a brief written report.

(*Option:* Instead of a written report, discuss with a partner or a group what you have done.)

END

54.   QUESTIONING

A   G   S   L

READ FOCUS: Structuring questions for maximum group response.

[It is a sad fact that many of the questions we ask other individuals inhibit answers more than they encourage them. Formulating a question so that a wide variety of responses are possible may take some practice. The examples below illustrate the difference between open-ended and closed questions. Closed questions are useful and appropriate in certain situations, but not where the maximum involvement of a small group is desirable.

Examples of Questions

Closed: Are we going to use majority vote here or just talk it out?
Open-ended: What method for resolving our differences are we going to use?
Closed: Should we fly or drive to the beach?
Open-ended: How should we go to the beach?
Closed: Should I buy that car?
Open-ended: What kind of car should I buy?

Open-ended questions present several advantages. They invite a wider range of alternatives and ideas, and they are likely to elicit a response from more people than are closed questions. Note that open-ended questions are multivalued while closed questions restrict answers to "yes" or "no."

Questions are opened up a bit by using indefinite language, thereby removing all prior assumptions, and by asking for an immediate response. For example: "What are your reactions to that?" "How do *you* feel about this?" "What do you think?" These are open-ended questions. With skillful timing, such simple questions as these can foster very productive responses, which can then be narrowed down to more specific areas for group discussion.]

DO ACTIVITY: 1. Practice phrasing closed and open-ended questions (one each) on the following topics:

Energy Shortage	Election-Campaign Reform
Congressional versus Presidential Power	Marriage
U. S.-Sino Détente	Wiretapping

2. Practice inserting the kind of open-ended questions listed above at an appropriate time in three or four groups in which you are a member.

DO ANALYSIS: Assess the outcome of both of the above activities. Are there any additional aspects of question forms you can think of that are not covered here?

END

55.   CLIMATE-MAKING

A   SA   S

READ FOCUS: Group climate and effects of climate on group interaction.

DO ACTIVITY: 1. Select one of the following "scripts" at the beginning of a new task in your group or at the first meeting of a newly formed group.

_____ Climate of hopelessness and futility

_____ Climate of warm camaraderie

_____ Climate of anger and hostility

_____ Climate of distrust and caution

2. Your goal is to create an atmosphere in your group like one you have selected. This is a difficult assignment. You may want to begin by trying out a form of behavior on a group of friends or relatives as a means of getting into the feel of "steering" your group's mood. Do your best to manage a "spontaneous" behavior in the group—to push it along toward the climate you selected without coming under suspicion. To do so successfully, you will need to enlist the *unknowing* cooperation of other group members—perhaps by reinforcing the contributions of those that strengthen the climate you are bent on creating. Do this for no more than ten or fifteen minutes.

DO FEEDBACK: Explain what you have been trying to do. Initiate a discussion for ten minutes on the following questions. How successful were you and why? What did members think about your behavior? If somewhat successful, what effects of this climate could be traced to subsequent group interaction? What is a group "climate" and what are some of its good and bad effects on group work?

END

56. MEET THE PRESS

G   SA   L   E

READ FOCUS: Communication in stress situations.

[We are often faced with high-pressure situations in which some of our attitudes and values are tested through interpersonal conflict. We have all experienced situations in which we have been outnumbered by people who assail our ideas and beliefs. In these situations many of us "fall apart," withdraw, or otherwise fail to mobilize our skills to support our position effectively. This exercise can serve as a dress rehearsal for a high-stress interpersonal encounter of this kind.]

DO ACTIVITY: Take a position on some controversial issue about which you feel strongly. Your position should be rather unpopular so that opponents of it will be easy to find. Find three who are opposed, but do not discuss the issue at length with them—only long enough to identify them as antagonists. Ask them to portray reporters who will question you in the "Meet the Press" style.

Arrange yourselves so that you as the Public Figure sit facing the three reporters. This is not a role-playing session, except for the aspects discussed below. Therefore, refer to one another with the appropriate form (Mr. or Ms.) and surname. Begin.

Reporters: You are not to engage in long harangues, but must proceed to attack the Public Figure by the questioning method, doing your best to upset, confuse, and embarrass this person. Put Public Figure's reasoning under a microscope and vigorously test his thinking.

Public Figure: You must do your best to handle these questions to the advantage of the position you are advocating and in a manner that maintains the best possible face or image. But remember, you are not responsible for answering unclear or poorly phrased questions nor for listening to speeches from the reporters. When this occurs, take the offensive and keep them honest. Your goal is to come across with integrity, a well-reasoned position, and sound thinking under pressure.

DO ANALYSIS: Stop after twenty minutes and discuss with reporters what you did effectively—and ineffectively. Discard the issue completely and focus on your communication strengths and weaknesses in this kind of pressure situation. Remember this exercise was not a contest over an issue. It was a device for practicing your communicative skills in stress situations. Solicit suggestions for ways in which to improve your abilities to communicate more persuasively and effectively.

END

C

Individual First Aid

57. SELECTIVE BEHAVIOR MODIFICATION
D   SA   S

READ FOCUS: Modification of a limited aspect of an individual's communicative behavior.

[We constantly shape the behavior of others during our interaction with them, just as others shape our own behavior. Often, this process occurs without our intent or knowledge.]

DO ACTIVITY: Select a partner. During the first few minutes of a discussion, isolate something in your partner's behavior—speech, manner, a gesture, an idea, a topic, and subtly introduce disturbing reponses when the behavior occurs. Again, identify in your mind some aspect of your partner's behavior that you would like to alter for just the duration of your immediate encounter. Then carefully respond in a manner to diminish it. For five minutes or longer, begin your schedule of selective responses. Use smiles, frowns, comments, eye avoidance, facial expressions, unresponsiveness, or whatever might diminish that target behavior until you find the most effective means for altering this feature.

DO FEEDBACK: Disclose to your partner what you have been trying to do, how you tried to do it, and with what observable effects. Discuss the behavior modification that goes on from moment-to-moment all of the time in interpersonal encounters. How do we accomplish this modification? Why aren't we more aware of it when we do it? How do we modify our own behavior in seeking certain rewarding responses from others? Summarize the details of this experience, including partner's responses, in a brief written report. Or discuss the activity with a partner or small group.

END

58.   IMAGE PRESENTATION DYADS

G   L

READ FOCUS: Messages "given off."

[When we interact with others we frequently have the desire to "come off" in a certain way—to leave a certain impression. We often use topics of conversation to present an image. In the words of one writer, we "take a line" and attempt to maintain our "face" through behaving in accordance with that line. We conduct ourselves in this way from all kinds of motives. At times we do it even without knowing that we are doing it—automatically and spontaneously. It might be beneficial to recognize this behavior in ourselves and also to recognize when others are striving to create an image for themselves.]

DO ACTIVITY: 1. Set an image goal for yourself. You are going to be talking with another person with the private intent of influencing this person to identify you with a certain desirable quality or trait. You must somehow communicate and behave in a manner that *subtly* conveys this image to the other person. Avoid transparency in working for your image goal. If the partner realizes you are consciously striving to act in a certain way, you lose your effectiveness immediately.

2. Write down your image goal—"intelligent," "likable," "complex," "shrewd," "sophisticated," "accomplished," "imaginative," "knowledgeable" —and put it in your pocket. Select a trait that is positively valued in our culture.

3. Pair off with a person who does not know you very well and talk casually for five or ten minutes.

4. Stop and write on your slip of paper what you guess your partner's image goal to be.

5. Switch partners with the nearest pair and proceed as above for five or ten minutes.

6. Stop and write down your estimate of your second partner's image goal.

DO FEEDBACK: Both interchanged pairs come together in a four-person group. Identify your guesses about the image goals of those with whom you have interacted. After all your guesses have been read, identify your actual goals. Discuss the following questions and individually write your answers to each:

1. Were you successful in your own image goal attempts?
2. If you were unsuccessful, why?
3. How did you convey the impression you did?
4. Are we all really this manipulative in our interaction?
5. What do manipulative behavior and image goals have to do with inter-personal communication?

END

59.   PROGRAMMED BEHAVIOR STRETCH

A   E

READ FOCUS: Trying something new. Widening one's behavioral potential in the group.

[We all nail ourselves into very tight behavioral boxes by our habits, our natures, and the unknowing help of others. In this exercise you will attempt to break out of your behavioral box, first gradually and then radically. You will use role-playing as the device, perhaps feeling a bit strange or uncomfortable in the process because, if you do this unit well, you will be moving outside of your boxed self-concept and "usual" behavior.]

DO ACTIVITY: 1. Study the Behavior Check List on page 149.

2. Identify those behaviors that most nearly describe your past conduct in small groups. Place an "S" (for Self) before each of these self-descriptions.

3. Identify the items that are exceedingly unlike your typical behavior in small groups, that are farthest from your range of comfortable behavior. Place a "G" (for Goal) in front of each of these items.

4. Identify behaviors that are about half-way between "S" and "G" with respect to their difficulty for you to perform. Place an "H" (for Halfway) in front of these items.

5. Go back over the items you have marked, and check to make sure that the "S" items fit you pretty well, the "G" items do not fit you at all and would be the most difficult for you to perform, and the "H" items are about halfway up the ladder of difficulty.

6. Over the next three weeks, find an opportunity in the groups in which you participate to incorporate the "H" items into your conduct. Incorporate

them where they fit into the interaction; that is, where your behavior will not be suspect. Perform this activity several times in different groups or on different occasions. Once you have mastered the "H" behaviors—have developed a facility with this range of behavior—you are halfway through the unit!

7. Now move up to your "G" items. Work on these individually or in some combination, using whatever stratagem you need in order to be able to perform them. Continue to practice these behaviors until you are somewhat at ease in performing them. You should be able to arrive at this point within at least three weeks after starting this excerise—if you are diligent.

8. Attend a group meeting with your goal behaviors memorized and be ready to spring them on the group members.

DO FEEDBACK: Without announcing it and in the context of your classroom group work, display your skill with each of your "G" behaviors. Afterward, announce your project to the group, and indicate that you have reached your goals and do indeed have a capability of producing them in the group. Solicit five minutes of feedback from group members on your proficiency levels.

END

BEHAVIOR CHECK LIST

Directions: "S" items are descriptive of self; "G" items are the most unlike self; "H" items are halfway between "S" and "G." Label each item accordingly. Items not fitting any category should be left blank.

_____ Constantly raises objections, bringing up old topic after group has dealt with it

_____ Interprets the discussion question

_____ Summarizes, integrates contributions

_____ Is receptive to ideas of others

_____ Gets things started

_____ Boasts, calls attention to self, relates irrelevant personal experiences

_____ Jokes and makes humorous remarks

_____ Challenges others' opinions

_____ Argues technicalities

_____ Contributes factual information

_____ Gets off subject

_____ Interrupts others

_____ Praises, encourages, supports others

_____ Uses group as audience for his mistakes, feelings, beliefs; ignores group task

_____ Makes deadlock-breaking suggestions

_____ Arbitrates differences of opinion

_____ Tries to get people to contribute

60.   MODELING

A   D   E

READ FOCUS: Imitating an effective communicator.

DO ACTIVITY: 1. Think of the best interpersonal communicator you have ever known. This person may be a relative, a friend or acquaintance, or someone around whom you have spent some time. Your model may or may not be someone whose ideas you like.

2. Without revealing what you are doing to those with whom you are interacting, imitate on at least three occasions some of the communicative behavior of your model.

DO ANALYSIS: 1. Analyze specifically what it is in the behavior of your model that contributes to his or her effectiveness.

2. Imitate your model on three more occasions, each time trying to emphasize or exaggerate those factors that you identified as central to your model's effectiveness while dropping irrelevant behavior.

3. Tell someone what you have done and together evaluate your modeling efforts. How far can you go toward integrating the effective factors of another's communicative behavior into your own communicative habits?

END

61.   THE BLITZ

G+   E

READ FOCUS: Analysis of communicative deficits and skill practice.

[It is a cliché that we know ourselves better than anyone else does. But we rarely take advantage of that fact and try to use the special information we possess about ourselves to improve ourselves. This indifference is particularly true regarding our individual problems with communication. In this exercise we will first locate a difficulty we experience in interpersonal communication encounters and then launch an attack upon it. We will not use special gimmicks or games but simply some help from our friends, a commitment to change, and an opportunity to apply whatever creativity we might possess.]

DO ACTIVITY: About eight to fifteen individuals can perform this exercise.

1.   Write down at least two problems you have with interpersonal communication that, if remedied, would improve immensely your communicative experiences. Describe them as succinctly as you can in writing.

2. For example, "Every time I get into an argument I sulk." "I'd rather bite my nails than say something nice about someone." Divide into three or four small groups and take turns reading what you have written. Listen to the communicative problems of the others and question each person until each statement is understandable to everyone in the group. Help each person in your group rewrite the two problems more clearly and perhaps more simply. To put down "I need to be more effective" is obviously too unfocused to be useful.

3. Read aloud the revised statements.

4. Select the *one* problem on which you most need to improve. This problem is your target. Identify the target for your group and allow them to further improve upon the clarity of your statement.

5. Redivide into different groups so that no more than two people are together from the previous group. Now, test your target statement for clarity, accuracy, and simplicity of expression. Help each person improve his problem statement in this way, and write down your own revised version if the group can improve on the original.

6. Taking each member one at a time, help that member find four different ways in which to attack his target. For example, one way might be for the member to observe someone who does not have the problem and analyze how that person avoids it. Another might be for the member to dissect the nature of his difficulties in a diary. Remember, the above are just examples. Your group should help you select four different approaches that fit your particular problem. List these approaches under your revised problem statement, making sure you understand what you are to do in each approach.

7. Carry out your four means of attacking your communicative problem, keeping a record in writing of all the attempts and their results.

DO ANALYSIS AND FEEDBACK: When you feel you have obtained all the mileage you can from these approaches, evaluate each experience and any progress on your problem. Report back to your group, discussing your own and others' experiences in this exercise.

END

D

Group First Aid

62. STRAIGHT EVALUATION FEEDBACK

G   E

READ FOCUS: Evaluating others; the effects of evaluation from others.

DO ACTIVITY: Privately, write down one positive and one negative statement
about each member of your group. You should be able to make these evaluative statements with little effort if you are paying attention in your group.
Now form into your group, and take turns reading your statements *without*
ad-lib comments, explanations, or qualifications. Move around the group until
everybody has read their statements. Do not discuss these statements; do not
comment on them; do not question them. When your group has completed
this phase, move to "Do Analysis."

DO ANALYSIS: Now devote ten minutes to each of the following questions in
the order in which they appear. Be sure to stick to the narrow area of each
question:

1. Ask any questions of clarification of other members' statements.
2. Report briefly and honestly your strongest feelings about the evaluations
   of yourself by others.
3. Discuss the differences in the language of different evaluator statements and
   any implications regarding the attitudes and feelings of the evaluators.

4. Discuss any nonverbal behavior of evaluators during readings, and relate these to their attitudes and feelings.

5. Where possible, relate statements of evaluation to your previous experiences in this group.

6. Identify any trends in evaluations and help with suggestions for increasing communicator effectiveness.

7. Kiss, and disband until the next meeting.

If each member has tried to be fair and honest, everyone should have learned something from the exercise. Assess in your own mind how the information from this session can assist in the modification of your own behavior in this group in the future.

END

63. NEGATIVE ROLE PRACTICE

G   S

READ FOCUS: Dysfunctional role behavior.

[Occasionally each of us lapses into behavior that is destructive to the best group work—anticreative, antiperson, antiproductive, defensive, and self-oriented. Some of our lapses are longer than others, and for some these behaviors are roles, a way of (group) life. But the destructive effects of certain behaviors are often hard to see, because they are interspersed throughout our social interaction with more functional behavior. We will now spend ten to fifteen minutes exaggerating the effects of some negative roles in the group.]

DO ACTIVITY: In five- to nine-member groups, cut out the slips on page 155, separate them, and have each member draw one "script" each. When the group resumes its discussion on its current project, each member is to follow the behavioral script he selected, remaining within the negative role described.

DO ANALYSIS: When interaction becomes too ridiculous to maintain any longer, stop. Talk it over. Did anyone see any "pieces" of himself in the behavior represented in the group? These are typical behaviors of unhelpful members, and we have highlighted and exaggerated them. They are examples of some of the destructive forms of conduct that cause groups to be ineffective or mediocre in their work. How can your group deal with these phenomena when they occur?

END

Talk continually	Be scornfully silent
Always attack people	Always attack ideas
Always agree	Talk continually
Always engage in personal anecdote	Always agree
Always make funny or satirical remarks	Grin only

64.   FIRST AID

SA   S

READ FOCUS: Development of skills to help a group move off "dead center."

[The group process frequently needs some communicative "first aid," and there is no nurse around to administer it. Here is an opportunity for you to develop one or two skills useful in any group, while simultaneously helping your group to move off dead center. Read this exercise through to see if it is applicable to your group at the present time.]

DO ACTIVITY: Pick one or more of the following roles to slip into when your group seems to evidence a need the role would fulfill.

"Energizer":   Move an apathetic, lethargic group into a state of dynamism, into some kind of forward motion. Utilize tension, play devil's advocate to spice things up, exude optimism and start others moving by any device that will work: persuasion, threat, coercion, pummeling.

"Supporter":   Boost a member that may need support, one who is dejected, tired, withdrawn, or being unduly criticized by others.

"Coordinator":   Pull some of the group's scattered ideas together, summarize them, and outline alternative courses for the group to take. Move the members on to the next phase in their task.

DO APPLICATION: These are all useful skills. Assess with a friend how well you did, how you could improve your approach to this skill next time around.

END

65.   ROLE INCONGRUITY

SA   S

READ FOCUS: Changing your role to "shake up" your group.

[For a variety of reasons, the task groups in which we work and communicate can become bogged down, lackadaisical, frustrated, or all worn out. It happens frequently and though it is usually a temporary condition, members feel it will go on and on and on. Usually, all it takes to drag the group out of the doldrums is for one member to zap it.]

DO ACTIVITY: If your group fits into any of the above categories, you can do something about it. All you need is a desire to improve the group's functioning and the courage to risk a little experimentation with your own behavior. Walk into the group on your next meeting prepared to present a new "face" to the other members—that is, plan a role in the group interaction that is *very different* from the one the group has come to expect of you. The two listed below are only examples, so use your imagination and go beyond them for your particular needs.

Example 1:   If you are usually the push-ahead, get-something-done initiator in the group, take a back seat and confine your contribution to supporting, questioning, and generally eliciting contributions and bright ideas from other members.

Example 2:   If you are usually a quiet or compliant person in the group, take a critical role and react to others' ideas agressively and critically by evaluating, probing, and questioning where legitimate.

Plan your role change very carefully and pursue it for part of a group meeting—long enough to provoke some curiosity, attention, irritation, or other signs of vitality and reaction from the group. Then revert to your former, more natural "self" if you wish.

DO ANALYSIS: Stop the group toward the end of your meeting and explain what you have been doing. Question the group on its thoughts during your "different" behavior. Lead a discussion of role expectations and their effects on the group, exposing what members expect of others within the group. Discuss also the ease with which a group's mood can be energized and changed for the better by a helpful change in a member's role—if, of course, you were successful!

END

66.   OVERPOWER

SA   L

READ FOCUS: Negative practice in leadership.
   [There are no exercises exclusively for group "leaders" in this book. It is unfortunate how use of the term "leader" tends to confuse group members as to their expected behavior, responsibilities, and attitudes. All group members may engage in "leadership," or can do so, whether they are called "chairman," "coordinator," "boss," "adviser," or just plain "Bill." It adds nothing to speak of a group "leader." A position may be created to facilitate group work, but the occupant of that position seldom has a monopoly on insight or on leadership behavior within the group. Through the device of role-playing, this unit demonstrates some pitfalls in overreliance on a single group member.]
GO TO PAGE 161 TO COMPLETE THIS UNIT.

67.   THE HIDDEN AGENDA

SA   S

READ FOCUS: Effects of a hidden agenda on one's self and on the group processes.

[The basic challenge of the small group is in engaging the various energies
and talents of its members and applying them effectively to the task before
the group. But a group is composed of unique individuals, individuals who
come to it with a variety of divergent backgrounds and from a number of different circumstances. If, at times, a member's behavior seems puzzling or at
cross-purposes with the group's direction and goals, it may be a function of
some special situation or state of mind incurred outside the group and perhaps even unrelated to the group itself. Such a state of mind has been labeled
a "hidden agenda." A hidden agenda might plague all of us at times. Depres-
sion from a specific turn of events in one's personal life; extreme fatigue from
loss of sleep, nervous tension, or irritability over an upcoming event or responsibility; anger at an incident on the job or in the home—all these are hidden agendas. They are just some of the internal states that can block group
work by upsetting interpersonal relationships among the members.]

DO ACTIVITY AND APPLICATION: 1. Be on the lookout for a hidden agenda
in your own behavior—something that has little or nothing to do with the
group you are in but which is affecting your contribution to the group.

2. When you realize that your behavior has been hindering effective group
functioning, stop the group for a moment and make your hidden agenda explicit.

3. Discuss briefly with the group the connection between your present
behavior and your hidden agenda, indicating your resolve to deal more realistically and fairly in the present group situation.

END

51.   ATTITUDINAL CHAIRS (Cont.)

DO ACTIVITY: Take a minute to recall the attitude of the member to your left.
For about five minutes, rehearse mentally what that person said and how that
person reacted to what others had to say. The ability to recall your neighbor's
position is related to how well you listen to others and your ability to empathize with them. You are going to trade identities for a few minutes and step
into the shoes of the member to your left. Remember, when you start discuss-

ing the nation's priorities again, you will be expressing the attitudes of the person to your left. So, don't just mouth the words, but model even your non-verbal behavior after the other person, communicating the feelings of the other as well as the ideas. In this way discuss for ten or fifteen minutes and stop. Now consult the person to your *right* and without arguing about the topic, advise that person on how to role-play your position on this issue more effectively— more effectively than he or she has just done. When everybody has received feedback and advice, begin discussion again for ten minutes more.

READ APPLICATION: There are several insights that can be gained from this exercise. First, you can find out how another person perceives your behavior and whether you have effectively communicated your ideas on a topic. Also, you may learn a little of what another's feelings and ideas are really like in this respect. It takes very little encouragement to listen to those whose opinions and actions we approve. The real test of an effective communicator (listener) is whether he gives the same attentive care to the ideas and opinions he detests.

DO ANALYSIS: Discuss ideas and feelings generated by this unit. Did you notice any room for improvement in your own communication skills and attitudes? How good a listener are you compared with others in your group? How could you improve?

END

52. ATTITUDINAL ROLE REVERSAL (Cont.)

DO ACTIVITY: Take a minute to study your partner's arguments and general attitude. You are going to reverse positions and put yourself in your partner's shoes. The extent to which you will be able to do this well is an index of your ability to empathize with others who think differently. Communicate with the same feeling that your partner expressed. For the next ten minutes, you *are* your partner and your partner is *you.* Attempt to persuade just as your partner did in the first discussion. After ten minutes, stop. Without arguing about the topic at all, hold an "advisory" conference with your partner, giving each other some pointers on how to portray your side of the issue more effectively and fairly. That is, school one another in some ideas to make both of your role reversals more convincing and effective. After this brief conference, renew the discussion in your reversed roles.

READ APPLICATION: This exercise is one way in which to gain a bit of insight into and empathy for the other's position. It also provides a chance to explore why the "other side" feels as it does without necessarily agreeing with it. It takes very little encouragement to listen to those whose opinions and actions we endorse. The real test of an above-average communicator is that person's willingness to give the same attention to ideas he deplores.

DO ANALYSIS: Discuss your feelings and ideas from this unit. How good a listener are you? How can you improve?

END

66.   OVERPOWER (Cont.)

DO ACTIVITY: Take over from the very beginning of a discussion and maintain control for fifteen to twenty minutes. Politely assume responsibility for certain decisions and the direction the group should take. Permit discussion, but manage to run the group and take over more of a share of group "leadership" than you or anyone else should. Do not insult others overtly, but keep your fingers in every group decision or discussion that determines the course the group will take. In short, assume the widest permissible scope of power in the group right up to the point of unacceptability. After fifteen to twenty minutes, stop the discussion and without explaining what you have been up to, distribute copies of the questions below to each group member.

1. Summarize briefly in a word or phrase what you felt about

_____'s method of running the group._____
     (your name)

_____

2. Explain briefly why you felt this way.

3. How do you think others accepted the way _____ behaved
                                              (your name)

in the group? _____ Same as you? _____ Different? What evidence do you have for thinking this way?

DO FEEDBACK: Have each member read the answer to Question 1. The results should tell you how well or poorly you role-played. Then initiate a discussion about the remainder of the group's answers. What can they tell the group about responsibility for group decisions? About member feelings? About your image in the group? About overreliance on a single group member?

END

IV
Strategies for Group Problem-Solving

A

Problem-Solving Procedures

68. GOAL DELINEATION

G   S

READ FOCUS: Operational definition of group's goal or task.

[Groups frequently begin a task before members really understand what it is. Much time and energy is lost when members have conflicting views about their group's goal. And asking them if they understand the group's objective is next to useless because they all usually feel they have a general idea about what they are going to do and they tend to persist in their private, unique interpretations over many hours of discussion. It takes only a few minutes at the outset of group endeavor to discover whether members have a common or a different goal in their heads, thereby avoiding much wasted effort at later stages of interaction.]

DO ACTIVITY: In a four-to-six-member group, have the members paraphrase what they believe to be the group's specific goal. If any members perceive more than one goal, let them identify the order in which they are to be tackled by the group. If all members agree in their opinions about the group's goal, quickly put it in the form of a written statement. If disagreement exists, discuss each member's statement until a consensus is reached. What will you have when you are done? Your statement on the group's goal may be something along the lines of the following: "A report documenting that the world is flat."

"Advice for the president on the spending limit for the company picnic." "A detailed flow chart on how to move the library into the new building with ordered steps and time estimates for each phase." The point is that your emerging goal statement must be clearly stated in simple language in a single short sentence.

READ APPLICATION: An operational definition of a group's goal is a specification of the concrete form its task will take, including the various steps in reaching the goal. Before you start a new task, it is helpful to know how you can recognize when it is accomplished. How will you know when you have achieved your goal? What will that achievement look like? This procedure takes only a few minutes and can clear up misconceptions that may exist at the beginning. It can also expose a poorly articulated charge given to the group. When you have finished this process, you should know your range of responsibilities and the scope of your power in decision-making on a given task.

END

69.   DECISIONS

A   S

READ FOCUS: Alternatives for decision-making.

DO ACTIVITY: Look very carefully at the following approaches to decision-making:

Voting:	Members cast open and secret ballots.
Compromise:	Contesting parties both give up something and get something they want in return.
Arbitration:	Other group members decide in interaction which of two or more rival ideas to affirm.
Consensus:	Rival positions are resolved through discussion to everyone's satisfaction.

Think of group situations in which each of these alternatives has been used. They are all appropriate devices to employ at one time or another. Some are more helpful in some situations than are others, and some are frequently used inappropriately—when a different approach would make more sense. None of them is perfect enough to be used automatically and unthinkingly all of the time and to the exclusion of the others, although some groups do operate in this way and to their own detriment. For example, have you ever been in a very small group in which must time and effort was used in self-conscious voting at the drop of a hat on every issue that came up? See if you can analyze the special uses—the advantages and disadvantages—of each method with respect to decision-making within the small group. Use the Comparative Decision-Making Sheet below for this purpose.

WHEN FINISHED, GO TO PAGE   197   TO COMPLETE THIS UNIT.

COMPARATIVE DECISION-MAKING SHEET

Advantages	*Disadvantages*
Voting	
1.	1.
2.	2.
3.	3.
4.	4.
5.	5.
Compromise	
1.	1.
2.	2.
3.	3.
4.	4.
5.	5.
Arbitration	
1.	1.
2.	2.
3.	3.
4.	4.
5.	5.
Consensus	
1.	1.
2.	2.
3.	3.
4.	4.
5.	5.

70.   DIVISION OF LABOR

SA   S

READ FOCUS: Special member roles.

[Before your group starts on a new task, you should raise the question, "Do we need any special role assignments for this task?" Special roles are simply one kind of division of labor wherein particular responsibilities are taken by one or more group members with the group's consent.

Groups need to be aware that they have the power to manipulate the group structure to enhance their work. This awareness includes the ability to see that on occasion a special role may no longer be needed. Here are some examples of special roles assumed by individual members:

Coordination of information of different subgroups or members working on different parts of a task.

Note-taking and summarizing.

Observing and reporting on group processes.

Reminding the group about time and agenda.

Representing the group interests to outside-of-group agents.

Obtaining specialized or technical information needed by the group.]

DO ACTIVITY: Take ten minutes at the beginning of your next group session to consider the special function arrangements listed above. Can you add to the list? Notice that most of these functions require only the part-time attention of a member, who is therefore free to interact as a full member most of the time.

END

71.   BRAINSTORMING

G   S

READ FOCUS: Introduction to brainstorming.

[Brainstorming, a much-used phrase since Osborn first introduced it in 1951, has been misunderstood by many groups.[5] It is often used as a synonym for an idea session limited to presentation of solutions in rapid succession. Actually, brainstorming is a two-step procedure. The first, or "idea," step—in

[5] A. F. Osborn, *Applied Imagination* (New York: Charles Scribner's Sons, 1951).

which members offer suggestions as quickly as they can—is often mistaken for the whole process. Brainstorming seeks to separate human reactions that usually occur in close combination. For instance, in many problem-solving discussions, ideas and solutions are criticized and evaluated immediately upon their presentation for whatever merit they have. Brainstorming, however, defers for a time all evaluation, criticism, and elaboration.

Step 1.

1. The problem is presented, and the group members think only in terms of solutions or partial solutions to it.
2. All solutions ideas are welcome, no matter how seemingly ridiculous or bizarre.
3. Members "hitchhike" onto the solutions of others by giving an idea a new twist, by shuffling around components of ideas, and by adding, deleting, or substituting new features.
4. Remarks are kept very brief—a short sentence or phrase at the most.
5. Members speak loudly so that all ideas are easily heard the *first* time.
6. Members refrain from asking questions about what was said or meant.
7. Members do not engage in conversations or criticize the ideas of others.
8. Members keep the ideas coming in rapid succession.

Step 2.

The second stage is very important. Here, solutions are analyzed for their potential, both in isolation and in combination with other ideas. Members match solutions, combinations of solutions, and partial solutions to the demands of the problem. Ideas are elaborated and explained. Useless ideas are rejected only after careful discussion and imaginative exploitation. The remainder are evaluated. Preferred ideas are selected, developed, and applied.]

DO ACTIVITY: Step 1: Following the rules and procedures above, pick a difficult problem of immediate import to members in a group of eight to twenty and select an "Enforcer" who will monitor your process. The Enforcer will keep members to the rules and start the brainstorming session. Position a tape recorder with a multidirectional microphone in the center of the group. If such equipment is not available, select two fast writers and have them coordinate all solutions on a blackboard. (If you use the blackboard method, do not wait for the writers to catch up, because any delay will undermine the value of the solution phase.) Go for five or ten minutes.

Step 2: Transcribe taped or written material for duplication and distribute copies to all members. Read each idea aloud and elicit explanations and extensions of ideas with merit. Make notes on useful ideas, modifications of and improvements on ideas, and new ideas that occur during analysis. Once a list of solutions has been devised, go back over it and select the one solution which has the highest probability of solving the problem. Or combine different solutions into a "package." Write a final solution, or solutions, into a paragraph report. Then, using your report as a guide, try to apply your solution.

DO ANALYSIS: Discuss these questions: What are some group tasks in which brainstorming might be helpful? What are some tasks in which it would probably be detrimental or useless? What is there about the nature of certain tasks that makes brainstorming useful in some cases and not so useful in others?

END

Β

Problem-Solving Attitudes

72.   PROBLEM AND SOLUTION ORIENTATIONS

G+   L

READ FOCUS: Problem orientations versus solutions orientations, associated problem-solving behavior, and probable effect on group performance.

DO ACTIVITY: 1. Divide into equal numbers of four- to six-member groups. Designate half of the groups as "Solution" groups and the other half, "Problem" groups.

  2. Select a complex problem of the multiple-solution variety (like a human-relations case study or a current social issue) and require a written group report on its solution from each of the two groups.

Instructions for Solution Groups: Begin discussing possible solutions immediately. After twenty minutes, stop. You have fifteen minutes to write a report that is to include: (a) your solution in as much detail as you can manage, (b) any necessary explanations underlying your solution or its application to the problem situation, and (c) how the solution would be implemented.

Instructions for Problem Groups: You have twenty minutes to discuss the problem. Devote the first fifteen minutes entirely to exploring the nature of the problem and its implications. *Avoid* any discussion of solutions as such. Use the remaining five minutes to discuss solutions. After twenty minutes have

elapsed, stop. You have fifteen minutes to write a report that is to include:
(a) your solution in as much detail as you can manage, (b) any necessary explanations underlying your solution or its application to the problem situation, and (c) how the solution would be implemented.

GO TO PAGE 198 TO COMPLETE THIS UNIT.

73.   TASK ANALYSIS

A   S

READ FOCUS: Sensitizing group members to the use of different approaches and different resources in dealing with a wide variety of group tasks.

[Groups are made up of individuals and, unfortunately, individuals are often "creatures of habit." Therefore, many groups are somewhat dogmatic and unimaginative in the way in which they attack their tasks. Quite often a group proceeds on assumptions that are unwarranted, assumptions concerning their division of labor, methods for problem-solving, means of resolving conflicts, and other features that form the group process. More often than not, a group does not even think about "doing it a different way." So, time after time, the group staggers forth, tripping over its own inappropriate and unexamined trappings. This exercise is meant to make group members more aware of the wide variety of approaches to group tasks, each requiring different uses of the group's resources. Different challenges require different methods.]

DO ACTIVITY: On the Analysis of Task Characteristics Sheet on page 177, list a number of group tasks requiring oral decision-making, tasks you have seen other groups perform or ones that you know about. In the space provided, identify five characteristics of these tasks that allow you to differentiate among them. For example, the task:

1. Had one right answer (or many potentially "right" answers).
2. Required evenly distributed member information (or large differences in relevant information such as technical or expert knowledge).
3. Had a result with an immediate or direct effect on members (or one without any effect).
4. Was a "one-shot" deal (or had several distinct parts).
5. Had many parts with no inherent order of attack (or had parts with necessary antecedents).
6. Was relatively open-ended so far as time was concerned (or the time requirement was explicit and short).

7. Required consultation with outside-of-group experts (or required no such consultation).

Also in the space provided, use your five characteristics as criteria along which to classify the tasks listed. For example, given the task characteristics of time, number of decisions required, and relation of solution to group members, a particular task might be characterized as "two-week deadline, 15 decisions to be made, and outcome directly and immediately affecting group members." The point is to try to see how differences in group tasks call for very different group procedures in order to complete the task successfully.

DO FEEDBACK: 1. Compare your classification schemes and the consequent task descriptions with those of others in your group who did this unit. 2. Conduct a short discussion in the center of the room for the benefit of those who did not do this exercise. 3. Initiate a discussion on "What implications for use of group resources or procedures do these different task characteristics suggest?" What ideas for alternative procedures can be made with respect to each task?

END

ANALYSIS OF TASK CHARACTERISTICS SHEET

Group Tasks

1.
2.
3.
4.
5.
6.
7.
8.

Categories of Task Characteristics

1.
2.
3.
4.
5.

Classification by Characteristic of Each Task

	1	2	3	4	5
1.					
2.					
3.					
4.					
5.					
6.					
7.					
8.					

74.   CREATIVE CONFLICT

SA   G   S

READ FOCUS: The creative and positive use of conflict within a group.

[Contrary to popular notions, verbal conflict in problem-solving groups is potentially a valuable asset. In fact, if conflict never occurs in a group, one should question if its members are alive, or if the group is doing a worthwhile job. Conflict indicates that group members are not inhibiting responses that may be unpopular. Unfortunately, when conflict does occur, few respond to it as an *opportunity* for creative work. Some group members even become depressed by conflict. But conflict means simply that people are different and think differently. Conflict is part of our society's political system, legal system, and economic system. From the dynamic tension and interplay of ideas that accompany conflict can come a new synthesis—a new idea to be tested by inquiring minds and rival passions. Somehow, many of us have been made to feel embarrassed or inadequate when accused of being argumentative. To which feelings we often respond with "We're not arguing, just discussing."]

DO ACTIVITY: The next time a disagreement of some import occurs in your group, stop the interaction. Go into a tight huddle with the two parties and inform them that the three of you have fifteen minutes in which to reach a substantial compromise that will be more farsighted than either of the two positions thus far expressed. Instruct the remaining group members to observe but not interfere in your triad and begin. After fifteen minutes put the position statement that emerges into written form.

DO FEEDBACK: Solicit reactions from the observing group members on how you did, how you might have done better, and whether there were any factors that preclude a more creative outcome from your interaction.

END

75.   SEQUENTIAL DISCLOSURE: CRITERIA

D   G   L

READ FOCUS: Decision by criteria. Formulating, testing, and applying criteria for decision. Cultivating the habit of forming criteria to guide decision-making.

[Usually more than one criterion is needed to guide important decisions. The following activity is designed to generate some insight into the process of formulating criteria for making decisions in the small group.]

DO ACTIVITY: You are going to have to decide which of two job offers, P or Q, you will accept. You must accept one of them, and you have only certain information on which to base your decision. The instructions below lead you through the following steps: (1) initial selection and ranking of your personal criteria for accepting a job; (2) reading additional information about the two jobs; (3) revision of your criteria necessitated by the new information; (4) making a tentative decision based on your revised criteria by circling P or Q; (5) repetition of steps 2, 3, and 4 for each of five sets of additional information about jobs P and Q. Begin now.

Step 1:

Select and rank your criteria for job selection (not necessarily limited to five):

1.

2.

3.

4.

5.

Step 2:

Job P	Job Q
We are pleased to inform you that we are able to offer you the position of serendipidizer in our company. This position involves a starting salary of $15,000. As a salaried employee in our company, you will naturally be expected to work on a job-completion basis. Please indicate your intention within the week as there are several other qualified applicants for this position who are waiting to hear from us. We feel fortunate in this opportunity to bring a person with your excellent qualifications into our firm.	We are pleased to inform you that we are able to offer you the position of pastramiologist in our company. This position involves a salary of $10,000 for the first year. We know that you can probably command a higher salary elsewhere, but expect our operation, thereby your salary, to expand substantially in the coming several years due to your addition to our staff and the carefully projected fourth-year growth in a small company such as ours. We will be able to keep this offer open to you until July 1 at the latest, but would appreciate your earliest possible decision.

Step 3:

Revise criteria:

1.

2.

3.

4.

5.

Step 4:

Circle job choice: P   Q

Step 5:

Read new information and follow the instructions below.

> After checking into the jobs a bit you have found that Company P is supercompetitive and advancement for the person of average talents is very slow. Job Q is with a small company with a great growth potential.

Revise Criteria:

1.

2.

3.

4.

5.

Circle job choice:

P   Q

> Company Q receives most of its profits from government contracts for research and development of nerve-gas containers. You will definitely have challenging work with Company Q.

Revise criteria:

1.

2.

3.

4.

5.

Circle job choice:

P   Q

> Company Q is a brains pool with at least half of its contracts in development of foolproof storage containers and disposal systems for a horrible nerve gas that is no longer being manufactured but for which the half-life is 500,000 years. Your involvement in Company Q might be exciting work. Your friends know that you are considering working for "the nerve-gas company" and are appalled that you would even entertain such an idea. Company P is one of the largest and richest corporations in the country and thinks nothing of working salaried employees an occasional evening.

Revise criteria:

1.

2.

3.

4.

5.

Circle job choice:

P   Q

Company P is a multinational which may offer the opportunity to work in Tahiti, Rio, Australia, Korea, and the Dutch East Antilles. Company P's top management consists of proven professionals who do recognize and reward excellent work with tangible dollar, stock, and promotion bonuses. You will never be able to influence Company P's policies unless you rise to the very top. Company Q is small and informal. Many Q employees see their company as an opportunity for hastening the day when horrors like nerve gas will be safely disposed of forever. As a new company, Q affords you the opportunity of "getting in on the ground floor" and hooking your fate to that of the company.

Revised criteria:

1.

2.

3.

4.

5.

Circle job choice:

P   Q

Company Q has no women in upper management yet, but is so new that this circumstance could be easily remedied. The future of Q is risky. Q could "go under" while P could not. Yet the signs are good for Q's future, its youth and small size notwithstanding. Company Q brings in Carl Rogers and other noteworthies to conduct an annual, weeklong, encounter-style retreat in Pago Pago for all interested employees and picks up the plane fare. Women actually outnumber men in the top management structure of Company P. P is known worldwide for the philanthropic P Foundation, which specializes in R and D grants to pollution-abatement and special-education programs. You know a person who works for P and likes it very much. P also has a number of free programs for employees and their families, including language classes, conferences, and volleyball, dance, and karate clinics.

Revise criteria:

1.

2.

3.

4.

5.

Circle final job choice:

P   Q

DO ANALYSIS:

1. Discuss and compare your final criteria.
2. Note how some of your criteria changed with new information. Should not good criteria anticipate new information?
3. Discuss the extent to which you used your criteria to guide your decisions.
4. Examine the relationship between criteria for decisions and new information. What are some other characteristics of good criteria? What value do criteria for decisions have once the decision is made?

END

76.   TIME STRUCTURING

SA   L

READ FOCUS: Experimenting with time. Planning group sessions and agenda with precise time periods.

[In the final analysis, all a problem-solving group has to bring to bear on its task are the resources of its members and the *time* to employ them. Time is the enemy and the friend. It's precious, irreversible minutes provide the framework within which we think, move, and interact. Time is so important that we take it for granted—never even thinking about it except in those frequent instances when, like money in the bank, it is running out. Time is a worthy object of some attention, some experimentation, and some planning.]

DO ACTIVITY: 1. Privately, plan in writing exactly how your group will use every minute of its time in its next session on your current task. You may include warm-up, socialization, or casual interaction periods in addition to the task work itself. But plan as precisely as you can each phase of interaction, the order in which they will occur, and the exact block of time that will be required for each phase in your group meeting. For example, perhaps several clearly identifiable aspects or parts of your task can be approached in sequence and separately from one another, each in its own block of time. Perhaps several parts of the problem can be tackled simultaneously by different subgroups and can be "put together" in an integration phase followed by an evaluation phase. You may even wish to include a division of labor in which members work in pairs on certain parts of the task and in the group as a whole on certain other parts. To do this unit you need the willingness of your group to experiment for one period of forty-five minutes. It should be emphasized that your time blocks are not "estimates." Once committed to this exercise, the group must stick to the time schedule with absolutely *no* exceptions; otherwise the values of the unit will be lost. In addition to introducing your one-session experiment to the group, you are responsible for keeping the group to the time schedule as you interact along with the other members. Remember that the purpose of the exercise is to provide some insight and ideas about the use of time. The effect of the rigid structure used here may be good or bad with respect to the specific task on which your group is working at the time.

2. Complete a copy of your time schedule for all group members and yourself, using the Time Schedule Forms provided on pages 187 and 189. Each item on your "Interaction Activity," list must be both brief and clear. Finally, note that two minutes are allocated in which you must obtain group cooperation and introduce the time schedules to all members. So, plan your remarks and begin the exercise.

DO FEEDBACK: At a later session take ten minutes and evaluate the exercise covering these questions: 1. Did the exercise at least make members more conscious of using time in a particular way? 2. Did the project open up some ideas about structuring time in different ways for more effective group work? 3. What were some disadvantages of structuring time in the experimental session? How can these problems be removed in a revised time structuring? 4. The time-allotment ideal for most groups on most tasks probably lies somewhere between the extremely rigid structuring in this exercise and the extremely sloppy structuring exhibited by many of our small groups. How could time be used in a way that retains some flexibility and at the same time permits some thoughtful planning?

END

TIME SCHEDULE FORM

Interaction Activity   *Time Block*

   1. Introduce "time structure" project   2 minutes

   2.

   3.

   4.

   5.

   6.

TIME SCHEDULE FORM

Interaction Activity   *Time Block*

   1. Introduce "time structure" project   2 minutes

   2.

   3.

   4.

   5.

   6.

TIME SCHEDULE FORM

Interaction Activity   *Time Block*

   1. Introduce "time structure" project   2 minutes

   2.

   3.

   4.

   5.

   6.

TIME SCHEDULE FORM

Interaction Activity   *Time Block*

    1.   Introduce "time structure" project   2 minutes

    2.

    3.

    4.

    5.

    6.

TIME SCHEDULE FORM

Interaction Activity   *Time Block*

    1.   Introduce "time structure" project   2 minutes

    2.

    3.

    4.

    5.

    6.

TIME SCHEDULE FORM

Interaction Activity   *Time Block*

    1.   Introduce "time structure" project   2 minutes

    2.

    3.

    4.

    5.

    6.

C

Special Problems

page 193

77. PROBLEM CENSUS

SA   G   L

READ FOCUS: Identifying basic assumptions; locating areas of agreement and disagreement; getting "behind" language.

DO ACTIVITY: In a five-to-seven-member group discuss an important social or political issue on which member feeling is generally intense and about which group members disagree. Discuss the issue until involvement reaches a high level and disagreements become more and more apparent. Essentially, this exercise requires that the group has reached an attitudinal impasse. Stop the discussion and appoint a coordinator who will show you how to use the Problem Census Sheet on page 193. The discussion should then be resumed while the coordinator sees to it that the following rules are carefully observed:

1. Only one person may speak at a time by making a short one-sentence declarative statement about the topical issue.

2. After each statement, each member must shake his head in agreement or disagreement. If one member responds in the negative, forget that statement. You cannot start this phase of the exercise until one member makes a statement that every member accepts (by head nod, one at a time around the group).

191

3. To achieve a consensus statement, it is best to start with a very general statement on which all can agree, a statement that can receive popular support in the group. For example, on an education issue such a statement might take this form: "Everyone in our society should receive the best education appropriate for that individual."

4. When a statement is acceptable to all, every member must write it down at the top of the first column on the Problem Census Sheet.

5. Write each consensus statement under the previous one in the same column. Once a statement has been written down, anyone may make another statement a little more specific than the previous one. Perhaps terms that are a little more specific can be substituted for those used in the earlier statement.

6. When a statement does not obtain *complete* acceptance, write it beneath the last one and circle it. Then start all over at the top of the *next* column with another abstract generalization that will win consensus. When you are finished you should have several columns of statements with the last one in each column circled. Your *overall* goal is to develop successively longer strings of consensus statements in each new column, where each statement is closer to the problem—more specific—than the preceding one.

    Feel your way gradually from abstract generalizations about the topic down to more specific statements at the bottom of the column. Try to learn from mistakes and to develop longer strings in each new column.

    Here are four other restrictions:

1. The only interactions permitted are the single one-sentence statement, the head nod (or shake), and a "please repeat" request in case the speaker's statement is inaudible. Even here the speaker must repeat the statement verbatim.

2. No speaker may be questioned.

3. No statement may be clarified or discussed.

4. No statement may be taken back or modified; it is either accepted or rejected as stated. If rejected, it must be written in the current column, circled, and another column started.

Begin now and continue until all columns have been used.

WHEN FINISHED GO TO PAGE <u>203</u> TO COMPLETE THIS UNIT.

PROBLEM CENSUS SHEET

1.

2.

3.

4.

5.

6.

7.

8.

1.

2.

3.

4.

5.

6.

7.

8.

1.

2.

3.

4.

5.

6.

7.

8.

1.

2.

3.

4.

5.

6.

7.

8.

1.

2.

3.

4.

5.

6.

7.

8.

1.

2.

3.

4.

5.

6.

7.

8.

78.   STIMULATED RECALL

SA   G   S

READ FOCUS: Reading between the lines within the group.

[Often we miss the opportunity to say something that we wanted to say in our group's discussion. Maybe we just could not get a word in at that point; maybe we withheld and then forgot a reaction or comment. This exercise gives each member a second chance, especially those who were less vocal during the original discussion. It provides all with an opportunity to voice ideas and feelings they failed to make known earlier. A playback of a tape-recorded portion of the discussion will remind members of some of those thoughts and feelings. Such *stimulated recall* should be used in connection with a decision-making or policy-setting discussion that is quite important to the group.[6]]

DO ACTIVITY: 1. Tape-record about fifteen minutes of a discussion that you know in advance could be of central importance to the group, that is, one involving a decision on the group's procedures, its task project, or the group members themselves.

2. After fifteen minutes stop the discussion, rewind and cue up the tape.

3. All listen to a replay of the discussion. Members are invited to stop the playback by pushing the "stop" button when they recall something they were thinking but did not say at the time of the original discussion. They are then to say their piece, permit a minute or two for reactions (if any) to their remarks, and resume the playback.

4. You are ready to begin. Place the recorder in the center of a tight circle, set the control for "record," and begin.

DO APPLICATION: When finished use any new data from the stimulated recall session to improve (1) the group's thinking on the issue discussed and (2) the group's procedures and interpersonal relations. Continue with your discussion.

END

79.   NEGATIVE BRAINSTORMING

G   S

READ FOCUS: Obtaining different perspectives on group methods.

[6] The process used here is modeled after those introduced by Dean James Clair, "Conscious but Unexpressed Thought Responses in Discussion Class" (Ph.D. diss., Northwestern University, 1955).

[Sometimes we get so used to proceeding in the same way in our groups that we develop a bad case of myopia. The present exercise may enable you to see your present group methods in a new and revealing light and at the same time suggest a change in some of these habits.]

DO ACTIVITY: 1. In your group (six to twenty) identify in writing a universal value pertaining to desirable characteristics of group process that no one in your group would dispute. For example, "All members should have an opportunity to contribute their ideas in the group" or "The group should use its members' skills and abilities to their maximum potential" or "Members should be rewarded for their efforts in the group."

2. Now, select a statement from the ones you have written which the group feels is the most important reflection of effective group functioning. Turn the statement around and phrase it as a question, BUT IN THE NEGATIVE. For example, a recasting of the above three statements might have the following results: "How can we keep member opportunities to contribute to a minimum?" "How can we assure misuse of special member talents and skills?" "How can we cause members to be penalized for their best efforts?" These are just examples. You are urged to select your own negative propositions.

3. Assume that after this training session your group members are going to disperse into other groups in our society for the purpose of bringing about a complete breakdown in the effectiveness of these groups. But you realize that you will have to be very subtle in your efforts to avoid detection. In your attempts to subvert these groups you may have to be a bit indirect in your suggestions and strategies so that you will not be classed as a "trouble-maker" and ejected. Therefore, all of your "moves" will have to be cloaked in a guise of respectability and good intentions.

4. Following the rules of brainstorming detailed in the unit on page 171, lead your group now in a negative brainstorming session. Try to come up with as many innovative ideas as you can in order to achieve your negative proposition. Remember to keep it moving fast, loud, and with short sentences. Remember also, to save elaborations and explanations until phase two. Have someone transcribe or tape record your ideas. Do this for about five or ten minutes.

5. Go over your idea list and clarify ideas for procedures and behavior which would subvert group effectiveness. Elaborate and add to the list, if possible.

DO ANALYSIS: Finally, compare each of the ideas on your list with present practice in your own groups and discuss. Are there current procedures or practices occurring in your group which parallel the items on your list? which have the same effects? Discuss ways to improve your group's functioning.

END

80.   PROBLEM AND SOLUTION SUBGROUPING

G   E

READ FOCUS: Helping group members with individual problems.

[For this exercise group members should have had some experience in interacting together in order for them to trust the group enough to be able to air their problems.]

DO ACTIVITY: 1. Lacking a more spontaneous method of selecting an individual problem to work on, use the following method: Have members in a group of from four to six write down three of the most difficult problems (regardless of their nature) they have been unable to solve. The problems should be the kind that make life less than it would otherwise be. They are to put their names on a slip of paper, and the name of one person will then be drawn on whose problem the group will work. Let that individual select one of his problems and identify it briefly for the group in writing.

2. Select two "Problem Specialists" from the group. They will help the target person see aspects of the problem he had not considered before. These members will *not* talk about solutions at all, just the problem. They will probe the target member to elaborate on the problem, its implications, its possible causes, history, and ramifications. They will then help him paraphrase his problem in writing in at least three or four different ways.

3. Select two "Solution Specialists." After listening to the Problem Specialists, the Solution Specialists will talk with the target member about solutions or partial solutions. Other group members must only listen at this phase.

4. Finally, all group members together select a solution and decide how it can be put into effect right away or tomorrow morning. Describe in writing both the solution and the plan for implementing it. The target member must then try some of the suggestions in the solution.

DO FEEDBACK: The target member is to report back to the group at a later date on his progress, difficulties, new attitudes, and so forth.

END

69.   DECISIONS (Cont.)

READ APPLICATION AND ANALYSIS: Answer the following three questions:

1.   Did you consider factors of:

Group time?

How official the decision "looks" to members of other groups?

How satisfied your members will be after the decision?

How willing members will be to implement the decision if necessary?

How interpersonal relations within your group may be affected by the decision method?

2. If you missed some of these items in your first activity, go back and add to the list of advantages and disadvantages.

3. Do you think any one of the methods is superior to all the others in most circumstances? Which one? Why?

On the basis of your reanalysis, make one suggestion to a group of yours to change or experiment with its decision-making habits. Persuade the members to weigh the alternatives before allowing a conditioned response to take over.

END

72. PROBLEM AND SOLUTION ORIENTATIONS (Cont.)

READ APPLICATION: Problem-oriented groups are those that use initial discussion time to get inside the problem on which they are working. They defer solution talk for a few minutes until it is clear that all members are "on target" and are familiar with the various characteristics of the problem itself. This period also gives members the chance to let off steam about the topic in question.

Solution-oriented groups, on the other hand, pitch in right away in discussing possible solutions before they have explored the nature of the problem and before they have familiarized themselves with any special aspects of the problem. In other words, solution-oriented groups assume a great deal about the knowledge and perspectives of their members, and from the beginning of their interaction the members talk simultaneously about the problem and its solutions. One result of this approach is that members of solution-oriented groups assume they are talking about the same issues when they are not.

Problem-oriented groups typically come up with solutions of a much higher quality than solution-oriented groups. They also often take more time to solve their problems than other groups, though this cost is usually more than offset by the caliber of solutions they produce.

DO ANALYSIS: 1. Print either "Solution" or "Problem" at the top of your group's written report, thereby identifying your group type. Without discussion, hand the sheet to the coordinator who will immediately shuffle all of them.

2. The exercise coordinator will then letter each report, beginning with "A," and read the identifying letter and the report aloud without any elaboration.

3. Every participant must now rank each group report for creativity, clarity and practicality, following the criteria noted on the Individual Ranking Sheet below. But do not rank your own group's report.

4. Taking one category at a time, each participant must now orally identify his rankings in all categories for each report so that the coordinator may record them where they may be seen (*e.g.,* on the blackboard).

5. When the coordinator has finished, help him total the ranks for each report in each category. (If the number of members in the groups is unequal, divide each total by the number of ranks given.)

6. Identify which reports came from solution-oriented and which from problem-oriented groups. Add total ranks for solution-oriented groups in each category and do the same for problem-oriented groups. You will then have two sets of ranks representing the two types of groups. The lower rank totals represent the better ratings.

7. Compare and discuss.

END

INDIVIDUAL RANKING SHEET

Directions: Rank the group reports in each column from "1" to "n" where 1 is "best" and n is "worst."

Group Report	Creativity	Clarity	Practicality
A			
B			
C			
D			
E			
F			
G			

77.   PROBLEM CENSUS (Cont.)

READ APPLICATION: When finished, you should have some useful information. The statements in the columns represent basic assumptions of the group, phrased in different ways. The circled statements reveal the actual area or areas of disagreement. The statements as a whole identify a certain common ground and range of agreement within the group. You should now have a common basis on which to build a more specific consensus or realistic negotiations.

Frequently, language and a rapid give-and-take hide the nature of disagreements. Differences on a topic may boil down to one or two concrete points, once excessive verbiage has been discarded. If you have done this exercise carefully, you should know considerably more about the viewpoints of other members than heretofore.

DO ANALYSIS: Using the following questions as a guide, analyze the language and other problems suggested by the contents of your Problem Census Sheet: 1. What differences can you find between material in the longer columns and that in the shorter columns? 2. How many distinctions were your members making in the early versus the later columns? 3. How can the top statements be described? 4. What is the nature of the circled statements? 5. Do the statements preceding the circled rejects represent the most specific agreements aired here? 6. What do you think your chances are for reconciliation or compromise of positions? 7. What have you learned about your own initial position in relation to that of other members?

END